Patient Poets

Illness from Inside Out

Perspectives in Medical Humanities

Perspectives in Medical Humanities publishes peer reviewed scholarship produced or reviewed under the auspices of the University of California Medical Humanities Consortium, a multi-campus collaborative of faculty, students, and trainees in the humanities, medicine, and health sciences. Our series invites scholars from the humanities and health care professions to share narratives and analysis on health, healing, and the contexts of our beliefs and practices that impact biomedical inquiry.

General Editor

Brian Dolan, PhD, Professor of Social Medicine and Medical Humanities, University of California, San Francisco (UCSF)

Recent Titles

Paths to Innovation: Discovering Recombinant DNA, Oncogenes and Prions, In One Medical School, Over One Decade
By Henry Bourne (Fall 2011)

Clowns and Jokers Can Heal Us: Comedy and Medicine
By Albert Howard Carter III (Fall 2011)

The Remarkables: Endocrine Abnormalities in Art
By Carol Clark and Orlo Clark (Winter 2011)

Health Citizenship: Essays in Social Medicine and Biomedical Politics
By Dorothy Porter (Winter 2011)

What to Read on Love, Not Sex: Freud, Fiction, and the Articulation of Truth in Modern Psychological Science
By Edison Miyawaki, MD, Foreward by Harold Bloom (Fall 2012)

www.medicalhumanities.ucsf.edu

This series is made possible by the generous support of the Dean of the School of Medicine at UCSF, the Center for Humanities and Health Sciences at UCSF, and a Multicampus Research Program Grant from the University of California Office of the President.

I am grateful to each of the poets represented in these pages for the various and surprising ways they opened doors to understanding illness. It was humbling and illuminating to work with their words.

I am grateful especially to seven remarkable women whose friendship and examples have taught me and many others what it is to live intelligently, creatively, and resiliently with long-term illness or disability. I dedicate this book to them:

Justine Blevins, Marilyn Chilcote, Mandy Dowd, Karen Fiser, Ann Metcalf, Annie Stenzel, and Heidi Wilson.

I am grateful also, as always, to my husband, John, who saw me through every page with loving encouragement.

Patient
Poets

Illness from Inside Out

for Heather and Logan
with continuing love and
admiration — *Marilyn*

Marilyn Chandler McEntyre

University of California Medical Humanities Press
2012

First published in 2012
by UNIVERSITY OF CALIFORNIA MEDICAL HUMANITIES PRESS
in partnership with eScholarship | University of California
SAN FRANCISCO – BERKELEY – LONDON

UNIVERSITY OF CALIFORNIA
MEDICAL HUMANITIES CONSORTIUM
3333 California Street, Suite 485
San Francisco, CA 94143-0850

Cover Art: Jen Shifflet, "Wishing On the Wind." Used with permission.
Design by Bink, Inc.

Library of Congress Control Number: 2012948247

ISBN 978-0-9834639-7-9

Printed in USA

Contents

Chapter One
Getting the News from Poems

It is difficult
to get the news from poems
yet men die miserably every day
for lack
of what is found there.
— William Carlos Williams, "Asphodel"

In *Reconstructing Illness*, Anne Hunsaker Hawkins provides a useful overview of narrative strategies in biographies and autobiographies focused on the experience of illness or disability, works that are now commonly called "pathographies." Those strategies serve very practical purposes. Two of the most common metaphors for the experience of illness are "battle" and "journey." Each of those metaphors frames and organizes illness narratives in distinctive and consequential ways. Since Hawkins' book was published in 1993 much attention has been directed to "narrative medicine," an approach to medical care that focuses on the role of narrative in the work of patients, physicians, and caregivers.

As a way of articulating and communicating the lived experience of illness or disability, poetry opens a very different window from narrative, emphasizing in its singular way discontinuity, surprise, and the uneasy relationship between words and the life of the body. The practice of poetry teaches us to hear words differently. Based on our training and what we learn to recognize as relevant to our purposes, we listen when patients tell their stories for certain kinds of information, and to expect it to be delivered in fairly predictable forms and sequences. When we break up those forms and sequences, we hear in new terms. Words, repositioned, reveal new ambiguities and affective possibilities. Familiar data may be reframed and lead us to recognize new kinds of relevancy.

Narrative is one way of hearing, delivering, and organizing information. Poetry is another. Both are mimetic: both give shape to experience with their own kinds of accuracy, and, even as they "mirror" it, they also "make it strange"—the latter the task of any artist whose work it is to help us see in new terms. It can be hard to remember that life isn't story. Things don't happen in logical sequence or unfold along well-constructed plot lines. Neither is life tragedy nor epic nor comedy, though each of those literary forms enables us to see something true about it. Every literary genre and work invites us to consider again how things happen—how we locate ourselves in time and space, how causes lead to effects, how we inhabit the present moment, and how that moment emerges from and reconfigures the past.

Poems set their own terms. If you want to read well and get the gift the poem offers, there are some prerequisites. You have to let go of the expectations you bring to story. You have to accept and dwell in ambiguities that do not resolve themselves immediately, letting meanings emerge, sometimes multiple possible meanings, simultaneously. You have to stop in odd places and reconsider your assumptions, and accept even the silences as invitation—as much part of the message as rests in music.

Patients who have written poems offer their caregivers unique diagnostic tools. "Diagnosis" in this sense does not mean identifying a disease so much as getting a more complete understanding of how the patient experiences disease, though sometimes a patient's image or phrase may actually lead to new diagnostic information. Poems offer both information and invitation. The information, however quirky, may be surprisingly medically pertinent—what hurts, when and where, with what quality of pain; how the daily tides of energy and well-being assume predictable patterns; what triggers anxieties and starts the adrenalin rush. The invitation is to open oneself to empathy, or to radical uncertainty, or to comic possibilities, or to uncomfortable intimacy. All good poems, even long ones, stop us as insistently as they move us onward. Every good poem has an undertow: as we read, we find ourselves repeatedly having to decide whether to go back, pause in place a moment longer, or move on to the next line.

In addition to information and invitation, good poems offer guidance. They offer alternative models or maps of suffering, pain management, adaptation, and healing work. It is helpful when reading poems in contexts of caregiving to consider each poem an answer to a question that deserves to be asked, and then to expend the effort it takes to identify the question.

A number of recent scholars have considered the question of how poetry works in contexts of illness and healing. In her 1999 article, "Poetry Breaks a Silence that Had to be Overcome: The Therapeutic Value of Poetry Writing," Gillie Bolton identifies some of the reasons why poetry writing in particular may be effective for patients (as well as for their caregivers): its initial stages "are often intuitive, and unreasoned"; revision of poetry, with its close attention to words, is often a process of discovery that brings "insight and consolidation"; it offers "a measure of control that can be stabilizing"; it invites speculation and inference in calling attention to what remains unwritten in the blank spaces as well as to what is written"; and it is essentially contemplative work." Therapeutic writing, she claims, is "an act of faith in the self" (Bolton, 119-121).

Illustrating that act of faith dramatically and explicitly, Barbara Neri offers a specific case study of poetry related to illness in her vigorous stage monologue, "The Consolation of Poetry." In the introduction, she reflects on her performance of Elizabeth Barrett Browning's poems—often undervalued and misread, she thinks—as an example of writing that is literally "a matter of life and death" (Neri, 46).

In that script, the character of Browning speaks as one whose life "is lived in full knowledge of death." The "Speaker" identifies herself as a reader who takes Browning's lines into her body as she reads, and feels "the reverberation" of Dante's vision of love and loss in them. The play articulates both reading and writing processes as exploratory work that fully engages the life of the body, considering numerous excerpts from Browning's poems as acts of survival, discovery, and correction, that make "pain into an art form" by precise, careful, subversive deliberation. Both Neri's play and Bolton's reflections, two among a range of scholarly and creative approaches to the question, insist on a complex, empathic view of reading and writing as work that literally involves the body as an instrument of awareness. Both insist, as many others have, on the specific diagnostic and therapeutic relevance of word craft.

One widely-read example of practical convergences between poetry and healing is documented in John Fox's *Poetic Medicine: The Healing Art of Poem-Making*, in which he tracks his work with hospitalized patients in writing groups, chronicling their interactions with each other, their struggles with the ways illness silences, and their efforts adequately to contextualize their stories.

The book includes a range of exercises recommended for readers who seek to explore for themselves connections between writing and the life of the body. The book is a landmark resource for students of poetry in medical contexts— not unique (similar experiments and studies have come out of several university medical centers), but more comprehensive than most.

Many hospitals now sponsor writing workshops like the Alzheimer's Poetry Project, founded by New York poet Gary Glazner, where caregivers work on the spot with patients to bring forth utterances that may be read and considered from the vantage point of poetics as uniquely valuable information about patients' cognitive processes. The Society for the Arts in Health Care (www.thesah.org) brings participants in such projects together at a yearly conference where experiments in therapeutic uses of poetry are regularly featured.

Such experiments may be seen at their most luminous refracted in the work of poet-doctors like Rafael Campo, who makes a similar case for the role of poetry in medicine, since it is "an expressive medium in language capacious enough to make empathy for human suffering, if not entirely comprehensible, then at least clearly and palpably evident" (Campo, 187).

The readings in the following chapters are offered as evidence for my conviction that caregivers can learn a great deal that is practical and applicable as well as surprising from patients' poetry. In this opening chapter I begin by considering three poems by patients about their experience of illness, pain, or disability, focusing on the kinds of information those poems provide, and on how caregivers may learn new techniques of listening from the hard-won words of people whose suffering has led them beyond the constraints of what narrative—case history or story—can fully accommodate. I will be focusing in particular on strategies of disclosure, the element of "confession" in poems about personal pain, the way images encode experience, and the function of the persona or point of view in poems where the distinction between poet and speaker is particularly sharp. All three are contemporary, all by women with considerable experience both in writing and in coping with illness.

Karen Fiser's "Still Life with Open Window," from her collection *Words Like Fate and Pain* recalls the pain and disorientation she experienced after major surgery (Fiser, 36). The poem's title, with its slightly ironic double entendre, situates it against a backdrop of visual art—one thinks of the many Dutch paintings of interiors with an open window that suggests a world beyond domestic walls to which access is carefully circumscribed, and of the "still life" genre that depicts "mostly inanimate subject matter." Another reading of the title, of course, is possible: the speaker still has a life; she is not dead yet. And there is an open window nearby that invites her to imagine a world beyond the hospital or sickroom walls, if not to escape them.

Still Life with Open Window

Pain, fatigue, hunger give time
the color of the infinite.
        —Simone Weil

I went to sleep as one woman—silken, magic, strong—
my life full of intelligence, bravura episodes
and turns of phrase. I woke up all stitching and sorrow,
with a silence around me like the endless quiet
at the edges of a late Rembrandt self-portrait.

Time spent in pain exists absolutely, without structure,
demarcation or relief, it is all one color,
like winter's rainy *sfumato* inscriptions on gray.
Meanwhile, the other, inner life goes on, unwitnessed,
the shadow a tree makes on the wall, rippling like water.

Since nothing outward remains to signify or to connect
one moment with another, no more achieved life
for the moments to be part *of*, they will have to be connected
by what can flower within the moments themselves.
Each moment must expand to hold my infinite, singing joy.

The epigraph, as epigraphs do, sets a frame: this is a poem about how pain changes the way we live in time. In *Space, Time, and Medicine* Larry Dossey documents remarkable cases in which a changed perception of time and one's own habitation of time proved integral to healing; escaping "strict linear time" enabled patients to come to new terms with their situations and literally find new energy for healing. Many patients experience a kind of timelessness that is both a function of pain and, paradoxically offers a way to relocate themselves relative to the pain and to lives in which pain will likely be an ongoing factor to be reckoned with. For most of them this project of relocation involves a stronger, clearer focus on what it means to live in the moment; that common word of wisdom becomes vivid and urgent as they turn it to a survival strategy.

Fiser's speaker moves in an orderly way from an initial observation about what has changed in her sense of her own body, to a reflection on how time itself seems to have changed, to a plan for adaptation to her reorganized life. What had seemed a seamless fabric, "silken, magic, and strong" has been torn and stitched and cannot be fully restored. A single, striking phrase, "all stitching and sorrow" takes the measure of how complete is the loss of what she once was. How things connect is different now: she will have to devise different ways of making meaning, different strategies of self-identification and self-love. Several poems in this collection and in another, pointedly entitled *Losing and Finding*, have to do with loving who she was before her illness, and the work of learning to love who she is after illness has wrought its changes.

But the poem is not a lament. It is a chronicle of process—orderly, dignified, deliberate. The degree of pain, or its location, whether it is sharp or dull, aching or burning, doesn't concern the speaker, but rather the way pain has reconfigured her habits of being: she has no navigation system to steer her through the fog of pain, and she realizes that she will have to work off the grid, foregoing familiar agendas, dwelling in one moment at a time, not seeking meaning in achievement or accumulation or progress, but in whatever may "flower" in moments that seem to be leading nowhere.

And this process is "unwitnessed"—a key term, since the poem itself discloses something no one can know or see without the speaker's own testimony. The image of the flower may evoke the lotus or the fiery rose that bespeak a contemplative journey inward rather than onward. Pain has taken away from this speaker exactly what some wisdom traditions encourage us to release: illusions that keep us bound in time and enmeshed in stories that obscure larger truths.

The poem ends not on a note of false optimism—the "nothing," "no more," "have to be" in the final stanza maintain the sense of loss and unwelcome necessity—but on a resonant note of hope that one way of living may be replaced by another equally, and perhaps even more, adequate to fostering awareness of the elemental goodness of being. Something has fallen away, but something has opened that may have its own sufficiency. On the other side of loss considered and accepted, the speaker retrieves a sense of an infinite, singing joy within, beneath the pain and more fundamental. That joy is not defeated by suffering, but will have to be channeled in ways more precise, limited, and intentional now, in the long aftermath. It emerges in the final line as a fact, not an aspiration. The authoritative declaration, "each moment must expand," suggests a resilient confidence that adaptation is possible. The conditions of the body's life do not determine the possibilities of the life of the spirit, though they make us revise our strategies.

One of the gifts this poem offers is the way it models hope. It frankly acknowledges the pain, the disorientation, the finality of loss, even as it moves with elegant and efficient grace to embrace the question, "So, how then, shall I live?" And the question is not a cry of anguish or of rage or despair, though it so easily could be. It comes from life-giving curiosity—a sense that whatever happens to change the life of the body introduces a new set of challenges to do what we are always challenged to do: accept what we must, assess what is possible, reframe what we thought we knew.

The speaker muses on her own situation with a precision and minute attention worthy of a good clinician. Careful, imaginative description precedes the decision about how to proceed. She finds a series of remarkable images to encode the experience, allowing herself and her reader to apprehend her situation as connected to art and nature—"unwitnessed," perhaps, but not unprecedented. The image of the inner life as shadow evokes an idea of the dead who live as "shades"—insubstantial, elusive, underground. The term "unwitnessed" compounds this sense: we all have some sense of being alive because we are seen.

What might once have been communicable logically and sequentially must now be approached by means of images. The darkness at the edge of a Rembrandt painting and the rain's undecipherable inscriptions of grey on grey and the insubstantial shadows of trees on water all suggest a dimension of mystery to be accepted rather than probed.

The speaker in this poem is highly self-aware, able to detach from her own pain and loss enough to make a critical assessment of what is happening to her. She opens with two sentences of personal statement that contrast the life she knew with what she has awakened to. As it turns out, awakening, in a larger sense, is just what she has done. As the second stanza broadens into impersonal reflection, the personal pronoun disappears: it is "the inner life" she speaks about rather than "my life." The simile, "like winter's rainy *sfumato* inscriptions on grey," makes pain a feature of the landscape, as ordinary and as uncontrollable as rain. Her situation has given her access to a truth larger than the facts of her own history. She has earned her way to the last line by doing the work required to accept, consider, and understand her pain.

We see a similar process of self-observation, chronicling, and imaging in Mary Bradish O'Connor's poem "Midnight Cancer" from her collection entitled *Say Yes Quickly* (O'Connor, 40). Like Fiser's, this poem offers an intimate view of pain, and focuses attention on how her disease changes the way she lives in time. The poem traces a circadian cycle, telling a story that has phases, but no trajectory. That the title is itself the first line of the poem contributes both to an ominous momentum and to a sense that there is nowhere to stand outside this experience: once the fearsome thing has been named, you are inside the fear.

Midnight Cancer

is a bottomless pit
where voices echo
around and around
endlessly
repeating the same
prayer:
oh
God
why
me?
Sooner or later, midnight
cancer changes to
morning
cancer,
brighter,
more hopeful.
Somewhere the sun
rises warm and round.
Birds are singing.
After a while,
morning cancer melts
into afternoon cancer
where it hides among chores:
cut the grass
clean the downspouts
drain the noodles.
Later, the house falls silent
and even the dog is asleep.
There might or might not be rain.
Without a sound

you are falling,
arms wide and circling.
It's midnight.
You have cancer.

Where Fiser's poem contains inchoate experience in three measured stanzas, this one seems to stop for shallow breath at the end of each short line. The short lines invite us to take in a phrase at a time, as though each partial thought occurs separately and requires its own burst of effort. A number of lines offer momentary resolution, but it is quickly dissipated; a following line will disrupt the temporary respite of a happy image ("sun," "singing," "noodles") or a period. The long single stanza suggests the relentlessness of an inescapable condition; though anxiety waxes and wanes, no real break is offered—no place to breathe slowly, take stock, find a fresh point of view.

The point of view established in this poem is one of its more significant features: where Fiser's poem begins and ends in the first person, O'Connor surprises the reader with the second person, inviting and even commanding unsettling identification with the speaker in a condition that might so easily be yours, dear reader. But she introduces that startling "you" only in the final line. Up to that point, "cancer" is the subject of each sentence. We are focused on what it does, rather than what the person with cancer feels. Feeling remains implicit, as though it is safer somehow to describe the experience in objective terms. So the "you" works to two purposes: it forestalls the more naked declaration, "I have cancer" by positing that claim as a kind of hypothetical: here's what happens when people have cancer. It also compels empathy: Imagine this. Enter into it. Go there.

The poem conveys an experience of illness that is not progressive except in its increasing familiarity. This speaker's accommodation lies not so much in reflection on the character of her pain as in close consideration of what makes pain and fear manageable, at least in the midst of the day's distractions. But every night brings its renewal of terror. The ordinariness of the day, and of the images associated with daytime—sun, singing birds, household chores—gives way to the uncertainties of nighttime ("there might or might not be rain") and a final image of panic, "falling, / arms wide and circling."

The terror with which the poem begins and ends is like a "bottomless pit" or vortex reminiscent of Dante's hell. Time, for this poet, may be measured by the welcome distractions each day brings, and the hours spent between those moments when the raw truth, "You have cancer," once again overtakes all the other occupations of the mind.

O'Connor, a therapist as well as a poet, died of ovarian cancer three years after publishing this book. In both this collection and another, *Calabash*, co-authored and published in the same year, she experiments with ways of getting at the emotional complexities of living with cancer. These include a poem that recalls a carefree childhood playing in streets sprayed with DDT, poems about the hospital, poems about grieving, and poems that reflect on the process of inscribing her illness in poetry. She also includes poems about others who are living with cancer, including her dog. All of these, as well as poems that remove the focus from the illness altogether, serve to contextualize a condition that has become a large but negotiable part of a much larger life, to be claimed and authorized, even in the process of dying.

A third poem that offers unusual insight into patient experience is written by a woman who lived for years with a constellation of undiagnosed symptoms until it was finally identified as a rare form of autoimmune disease something like lupus. Mandy Richmond Dowd's "Out in the Sun the Busy Lives Swirl" seems to present a case on behalf of a person who can't control the disruptive symptoms or the sudden pain-induced outbreaks that make social contact precarious and embarrassing. Where O'Connor's poem records persistent fear, this one testifies to the element of shame that so often accompanies illness.

Out in the Sun the Busy Lives Swirl

Sometimes it just gets in her hand, the shaking shaking
then jumps to her head like a train jumping track
and all the cars careen and none of the rules apply
Another lawless seizure on the loose

Sometimes she can hold it in one finger for a whole day
or if it grows big can give it to her foot

till her back will grab it grab her tongue too
and like a stubborn mute she'll try to tell you anyway, anything

cause everything is important in the moment
everything as urgent as the claw inside her skull
urgent as speech to the captive

A shock like a fist to the back of her head cracks
a whip in her spine and she's sorry she's sorry
for her biology, for her persistent wish to endure
the broken existence she's put in your path

And for the fact of her need she wants to scurry
like a hermit crab into the shadows
like a hobo away from the wedding
where none can rebuke the ungainly scope

of her ache
for a call in the dark from an old friend who sees
through the frightening symptoms of nature's frank and random course
the soul is the same is the same

Fear, longing, shame, and urgency characterize the speaker's daily life. The poet's choice to write in the third person allows her to align herself with the reader as outside observer—one who is learning about a pain whose course is unpredictable, and whose emotional repercussions run their own gamut. Fear of exposure, fear of being judged or misunderstood seem to drive the speaker with her urgency to explain and apologize; it is a plea for understanding that funnels its anxious energies into the poignant, insistent last line: "the soul is the same is the same." As in the other two poems, the speaker in this one is acutely aware of a growing chasm between the life she lives in her body and the "busy lives" "out in the sun." In contrast to theirs, hers is lived in a dark and secret place, to which she "scurries" and hides and waits for the one who "sees."

When I asked a disabled woman once what were the hardest things about being confined to a wheelchair, she immediately answered, "Very few people make sustained eye contact. They glance at you and look away." She went on to explain what efforts it took to escape the constraining social category of "disabled person." Dowd's poem enacts that effort, invoking what Francis Ferguson called the "histrionic imagination," challenging readers to think with their bodies and to identify with one who is like us, but has been invaded by an alien that performs its strange antics in her hand, her head, her foot, her tongue.

The poem offers considerable information about the speaker's experience of her illness and about her pain management strategies. The speaker responds to "random," unpredictable seizures in two conspicuous ways. First, she finds exculpatory images that absolve her of responsibility for what she knows to be socially unacceptable: what is happening in her body is "like a train jumping track." It is "lawless" and "on the loose"—beyond control by the rational, observant, inventive person who speaks of it—and herself—in the third person. It roams and grabs, pins her into a corner and knocks her in the head. Possibly the most jarring image is the "claw inside the skull" that scratches against barriers, trying to open a window to the world. A second prong of her response to the onslaughts of her condition is strangely and sadly confessional. Imagining how others see her, the speaker compares herself to a "hermit crab in the shadows," a "hobo" at a wedding, "ungainly" and out of place, someone whose "broken existence" is an impediment to others. These self-shaming images and the repeated apologies—"she's sorry, she's sorry for her biology / for her persistent wish to endure…"—have an ironic edge. They bespeak both authentic humiliation and a certain defiance: she has, after all, demonstrated that she has no choice about the "broken" body she inhabits. Her condition is her "biology," and her "wish to endure" elementally, rightfully human, even heroic, under the circumstances.

The absence of end-punctuation throughout the poem underscores its tentative, experimental quality. The speaker is venturing a try at making herself understood. But the two anxious repetitions work like an undertow that subverts her urgency and energy to liberate herself from isolation: "she's sorry, she's sorry," yet can't we see that "the soul is the same, is the same."

Poems like these can, if we let them, teach us to listen more imaginatively, more acutely, more compassionately. We can learn to attend to their images, their puzzling line breaks, their shifts of focus—to all the techniques we call "literary"—as keys to conditions of body and mind that could not be adequately articulated in any more discursive way. Suffering is a truth that must be told "slant," as Emily Dickinson advised. It can be conveyed, but not in simple declarative sentences, and not on scales of one to ten. The skills and discipline poetry teaches are transferable to the clinical encounter. Everyone who speaks encodes. All dialogue has its pauses, metaphoric detours, apparent irrelevancies, subtexts, allusiveness. Poems have many non-utilitarian uses, and I would be the last to recommend a simply utilitarian approach to them, but I do want to close with a strong, somewhat utilitarian claim: poems have practical value. Reading them well is praxis, and practice for the challenging, subtle, peculiar, rewarding work of reading what is inscribed in the human faces and voices and bodies that come into our clinics and classrooms in the hope of being healed.

Chapter Two
Insider Diagnosis

This hour I tell things in confidence,
I might not tell everybody, but I will tell you.
— Walt Whitman, "Song of Myself"

Prolonged or recurrent pain confers its own kind of authority. Strategies of coping may be refined over time, as patterns of pain, fatigue, and mood swings grow more familiar: patients come to know themselves in surer ways. Their answers to the recurrent query, "How are you?" may grow more subtle, complex, or ironic, and their descriptions of inner states more precise. At the same time, certainty that pain will return, that life without this particular suffering is unlikely to be restored, leaves its own residue of frustration or fear, inclining some patients more actively to resist well-meant messages of hope for cure or relief. Those who have weathered seasons and cycles of suffering know in ways that can only be taught by traveling that road what works, what is needful when, and the hollowness of certain conventional strategies of comfort.

The particularity and peculiarity of a patient's grasp of his or her condition may sometimes be most satisfactorily articulated in a metaphor or image, discovered and adopted as a device that bypasses rational explanation and conveys a holistic sense of the patient's experience. Finding the image or metaphor that "fits" the experience can offer both relief and pleasure. An apt metaphor opens a wide door to understanding, that can open onto a whole landscape of information. If, for instance, a patient alludes repeatedly to images of drowning, being overwhelmed, being submerged, then healing will need to be a process of surfacing or re-emergence. If their images are of brokenness, healing will require some sense of being put back together, made whole. Images of scattering imply a desire for gathering or re-integration. Images of contamination a desire for purification. In all cases, patients' images, whether intentional or unconscious, help to shape their understanding of their own conditions, and their participation in healing.

In his poem, "The Patient," Peter Meinke works his way through several plausible metaphors before arriving at one whose logic he unfolds in a final stanza, as though all the others only approximated the precision the last one achieves (Meinke, 4). All the metaphors alighted on and left along the way, however, inform and enrich the final one:

The Patient

disease has expanded my horizons
and pain
spread the good word

since I've been sick
I feel close to the blighted things of nature
(I myself am a blighted thing of nature)
 burnt oaks
 gutted houses
  (for surely houses are as natural as beehives)
 broken foxes lying by the highway

 bugs crawl along the rims of my glasses
 my body pocked with spiraled holes
 like those punched in butter
 in each hole something moving

hooked on disease (it gives
meaning to my life) I wriggle wormlike
around the pain and God
is the large-mouthed bass circling
below me.

The opening claims that disease has expanded the speaker's horizons and pain "spread the good word" invite us to consider how they may have accomplished those happy changes. Both claims may strike us as paradoxical, if not glib, at the outset, since disease and pain are more frequently associated with contraction, withdrawal, isolation, and bad news. The second stanza deepens the paradox: the expansion of consciousness has come about by deeper identification with "the blighted things of nature"—an identification made absolutely explicit in the parenthetical aside that insists we imagine the speaker in just this way to understand his plight.

The series of metaphors begins with one that has dignity and history: the burnt oak recalls figures of ravaged power like Oedipus at Colonus or King Lear who even in their age and debility maintain vestiges of grandeur. There is sadness in the charred tree, but also a certain tragic beauty. It stands as a testimony to how forces of nature always work at cross-purposes within a larger economy where life and death are coterminous. The image has a largeness to it that corresponds to the idea that disease has "expanded" and "spread" the speaker's awareness of himself and the forces at work upon him.

The second metaphor, "gutted houses," sounds a more desolate note, less tragic than simply sad. Event the ugly onomatopoetic effect of "gutted" downshifts from a certain awe in the face of the forces that wreak destruction to a more monochromatic sadness at the prospect of a vacant once-inhabited place. To compare the house to a beehive reinforces a certain ambiguity about the loss: the wax combs of bees, perfectly suited to their purpose, and durable for a season, are destroyed and rebuilt in the course of other seasons, and of their adaptations to natural pressures, including human management. To compare the sick self to the gutted house is recognize a sense of having been emptied, the business of living now taking place elsewhere, wind sweeping through the open places and grasses growing through cracks in cement. What was once of practical, even essential value now awaits a bulldozer—or perhaps a craftsman with the skill and resources to bring about restoration. It is an image that suggests age and loss, but also the quiet resignation that resounds in the opening lines of Eliot's "East Coker":

In my beginning is my end. In succession
Houses rise and fall, crumble, are extended,
Are removed, destroyed, restored, or in their place
Is an open field, or a factory, or a by-pass.
Old stone to new building, old timber to new fires,
Old fires to ashes, and ashes to the earth
Which is already flesh, fur and faeces,
Bone of man and beast, cornstalk and leaf.
Houses live and die: there is a time for building
And a time for living and for generation (Eliot, 23)

The echoes of the gutted house extend back to Ecclesiastes with its reminder that there is "a time to every purpose under heaven" that includes both "a time to break down" and "a time to build up" (Eccl. 3:1). So sickness has its place in the order of things.

The third metaphor descends further from the somber beauty of the first: "broken foxes lying by the highway" incite neither awe nor wistful resignation, but a reluctant confrontation with modern death where creatures are killed not by their natural predators, but by speeding cars on roads that cut through their habitats the way carcinogens and leeching petrochemicals invade bodies whose natural defenses are not designed to cope with them. The fox's native shrewdness has been trumped by the machine, its body on the road a reminder of the pyrrhic victories of progress.

Finally the speaker imagines his body as a corpse, riddled with bugs and worms, an image of decay where human life has been displaced by the busy life forms that dispose of what remains. Then he comes to the final metaphor: he himself is like a worm on a hook, whose life has meaning in its last wriggling agony, as it awaits the being it will feed, in whose belly it will be digested and transformed.

The poem insists on its own process of successive confrontations of the most challenging facts we have to face: that illness presages death; that the body will diminish and decay; that we are implicated in a pattern far larger and purposes greater than we can fathom, pierced, dangled, sacrificed, and consumed in a process we only dimly trace in our human ways of knowing. The speaker's authority lies in his willingness to undertake that exploration of what illness betokens. Therein he wins the right to his opening claims, and to an acceptance that cannot be glibly imparted, and can only be honestly achieved by "a full look at the worst."

Linda Pastan's poem, "Migraine," like Meinke's, conspicuously avoids the conventional narrative trajectory from onset to relief or recovery, but moves slowly through an inventory of pain sensations, emerging at the end only with a carefully tentative and hypothetical vision of what relief might look like: "silence or sleep/ or the cotton wool/ of the perfected dark" (Pastan, 68). It is certainly not the first of its kind; Emily Dickinson, Lewis Carroll, Jorge Luis Borges, and many other writers suffered from migraines and wrote about them, directly and indirectly, in poetry, fiction, and prose. The considerable corpus of Pastan's own poetry includes a number of poems that offer perspectives on pain, including one about childbirth in which the speaker lies in a room "where pain winces off the walls like too-bright light." "Migraine" offers no particular hope for cure, only for understanding; "headache" covers a broad spectrum. This one is not trivial. The poem offers a more adequate answer to the question so often asked of patients in pain: "On a scale of 1 to 10, how bad would you say it is?" In a sense, the poem is an indictment of such clinical shorthand—an insistence that pain like this deserves words, images, time, attention, breath.

Migraine

Ambushed by
pins and needles
of light . . . by jagged

voices . . . strobes . . .
the sanctuary is taken
from within.

I am betrayed by
the fractured
senses. I

crouch on the
tilting floor of
consciousness, fearing

the eggshell
skull won't hold, will crack,
as the lid is tightened

another implacable
inch. I would banish every
blessing—these shooting

stars . . . the future . . .
all brilliant
excitations—just for

silence or sleep
or the cotton wool
of the perfected dark.

The opening lines are short—almost breathless—in a way that characterizes what one critic called "emaciated poetry" whose lines, though they qualify as free verse, are "not free, but rigid" (Prunty, 90). Though that may be a rather harsh characterization of a technique that serves a number of purposes, including foregrounding image rather than statement, the lines do effectively dramatize a process of grasping for adequate images—the ellipses following "pins and needles of light," "jagged voices," and "strobes," suggest either hesitancy over the adequacy or precision of the images, or the possibility of more. The list is incomplete or insufficient, but abandoned as the speaker turns to a summary statement: "The sanctuary is taken from within." The idea of sanctuary develops the opening image of the sufferer as a fugitive whose last hope of protection from attack has been shut down by an alien force. The idea of going inward is common to descriptions of migraine; many describe the general experience as one of entrapment in an enclosure. Here, more complexly, the "interior" is perceived as a place of refuge—indeed, a last resort—that has been overtaken, so that a sense of betrayal is added to the feeling of entrapment. The passive voice, "is taken," emphasizes the anonymity of the aggressor, an inchoate, menacing presence that can't be identified and against whom there is no remaining defense.

The opening words of the third stanza, "I am betrayed . . ." reemphasize the dimension of hurt and outrage that accompany invasive pain in what seems to be the self's most intimate space. Though the "invader" remains unspecified, the source of betrayal is identified: it is the senses, the five vanguards of understanding, orientation, and empowerment, that have forsaken their assigned work. Vision is altered or disrupted by auras; light itself—ancient image and evidence of blessing—is painful. Olfactory hallucinations, a common feature of migraine auras, introduce their own confusion. (As a longtime veteran of migraines, I can testify to the strange reality of such hallucinations, having sent my husband on repeated futile trips to the kitchen to see if gas was escaping from the oven.) Sometimes one longs for touch, only to find even gentle attempts at soothing massage painful or irritating. Similarly, even the gentlest sounds can ratchet up the pain; even water or sweet tea can be bitter. One becomes desperately aware of these losses: what is one to count on, if the five receptors of all earthly comforts are "fractured" like broken bones that bear no weight?

The stanza ends with a lonely personal pronoun, contrasting poignantly with the "I" at the beginning of the stanza that is still a subject capable of a verb, capable of outrage and driven by a sense of self. The stanza break visibly reinforces the sense of brokenness, adding to it isolation and disconnection from the more intact "I" that has thus far narrated the experience.

The verb that follows indicates a dramatic loss of energy: the speaker has descended from forthright accusation of betrayal to the posture of a hunted animal, crouching on a "tilted floor"; she inhabits an inner space that has undergone something like the disruption of an earthquake: the foundations haven't held, and the edifice seems to be sliding. The short stanza begins with the physical posture and ends with the emotional sensation it betokens: body and mind are reduced by fear to a consuming sense of precariousness, corresponding, in an experience that many others have described, to the feeling that if one moves an inch in any direction the pain will stab in a new place or intensify.

The fear deepens: with the shift from a tilting floor to a skull thin as an eggshell, the sense of precariousness is compounded by an image of poignant fragility. The creature inside could die from one blow. The one protection that lies between the throbbing brain and the unbearable pressures of light and sound seems no longer capable of withstanding the slightest pressure. That pressure, shifting metaphors again, seems, again, menacing and intentional. Some ruthless hand is tightening a lid, the way one might trap an insect in a Mason jar. That the hand is "implacable" deepens the sense that the source of pain is impervious to all strategies—deep breathing, relaxation, medication, music, or even graceful acquiescence.

It is worth pausing here to note this shifting of metaphors in the poem. Each of them introduces its own logic, and its own dimension of the experience. Each adds to the thickness of a description that both specifies and scatters; cumulatively they suggest how the sensations of a wracking migraine defy singular representation. Each image gets at something true, but none seems quite adequate. This sense that there's no way to "capture" or even "tell" one's pain is common to the literature of suffering, reminding readers and hearers that every record of pain is partial, and all are translations from the language of that place Susan Sontag called "The Kingdom of the Sick," and Flannery O'Connor called "a far country."

At what seems its nadir, Pastan's poem takes a turn into clarity and resolution, even though only hypothetical and fantastic. "I would banish every / blessing" recalls extravagant and desperate language of banishment from Shakespeare—Romeo's "Hence banish'd is banish'd from the world / and world's exile is death," for instance. Or Falstaff's final plea to his patron and playmate now distant, rejecting, and harsh: "Banish plump Jack, and banish all the world!" Determined and resolute as the reformed Prince Hal, this speaker holds herself ready, in extremity, to banish "every / blessing," assuming the extravagant stance of a warrior making a last stand. She is willing to pay almost any cost for relief: the matter presents itself as a life-or-death choice, even at the risk of seeming melodramatic. The point is made and emphasized that in the moment, pain like this defies the rational knowledge that it will run its cycle and diminish, that it is temporary, that life and health are not seriously endangered. The tension between those facts about migraine and the experience of it charges the final lines with darkly comic irony that deepens as the list of imagined forfeitures expands to include the heavens, the future, and all promise of excitement. (Curiously, "these shooting stars" and "brilliant excitations" could also allude to the very sensations of light and exquisite, painful sensitivities or the speaker's current state, so blessing becomes strangely confused with exotic manifestations of pain.)

The wish at the end is hardly commensurate with such elaborate negotiation or costly offerings: silence, sleep, enshrouding darkness carry their own baleful ambiguity. Comfort seems contiguous with the obliteration of "sweet death" rendered so beautiful by Bach in "*Komm, süßer Tod*" and echoed in generations of death poems. Though not a life-threatening condition, migraine can, as this poet and others testify, bring one to the brink of death if only in imagination, and impart its dark gift like that of the thirteenth fairy in old tales, an intimation of mortality that opens up inner spaces like caves and reshapes the life of a mind left quite intact, perhaps, but shadowed by a lingering awareness of how provisional are the terms on which we get to live a pain-free day.

Jane Kenyon's "Now Where" provides a record of prolonged and recurrent depression that is in some ways similar to Pastan's representation of recurrent pain (Kenyon, 164). She suffered from, and took medication for, depression for most of her adult life. In both poems the source of suffering is vaguely identified as a malevolent other that invades, shadows, and sadistically invents new ways to torment the sufferer, following her into her most intimate domains and depriving her of hope for escape or refuge. In both, as well, the inner space is what we have learned to identify as the locus of self: the head, the brain, the mind, the site from which the conscious, self-conscious "I" sees and maps the world. Yet the "it" and the "I" remain separate, implying that there is a deeper, perhaps healthier, more grounded "self" that can witness and assess the effects of the lurking "other" on the self who suffers. This duality is common in patient descriptions of depression. Illness and pain often have the effect of splitting consciousness. One of the most common situations in which we may see this is in patients who self-report, often calmly describing their own anxiety, panic, hysteria, desperate sense of confusion, or pain.

Now Where

It wakes when I wake, walks
when I walk, turns back when I
turn back, beating me to the door.

It spoils my food and steals
my sleep, and mocks me, saying,
"Where is your God now?"

And so, like a widow, I lie down
after supper. If I lie down
or sit up it's all the same:

The days and nights bear me along.
To strangers I must seem
alive. Spring comes, summer;

cool clear weather, heat, rain. . . .

The speaker here is one who is being stalked, tormented, mocked, and finally driven into passivity and a sort of paralysis in the face of what feels like futility. The actual symptoms enumerated in the poem are clear and classic: a persistent sense of oppressive presence, or even slight paranoia; lack of appetite; fatigue; despair; sense of futility; dissociation between interior sense of self and social persona. Each three-line stanza is its own lament; not insignificantly, the form echoes the *terza rima* Dante used to walk us through hell. In the third stanza we also hear an echo of Ecclesiastes' "all is vanity" in the profound indifference that leads to the feeling that "it is all the same," no matter what action one takes.

One of the more poignant moments in the poem comes in the phrase "like a widow." The speaker presents herself here as a person who has suffered a loss of an essential relationship, loss of love energy, loss of daily conversation. Her depressions were, in fact, exacerbated by actual fear of widowhood in the wake of her husband's cancer diagnosis. Ironically enough, though he was 19 years older than she, he outlived her. But his illness, before hers, shadowed their marriage and her poetry. Much of her poetry is about loss or potential loss as a feeling—a dread, an ambient heaviness, an inchoate sense of possibility, represented in two curious lines from a poem in her last collection, "Afternoon in the House": "I know you are with me, plants / and cats—and even so, I'm frightened / sitting in the middle of perfect / possibility" (Kenyon, 47).

To see depression as loss is to move beyond a clinical understanding to a larger and less definable grasp of it as a spiritual condition. Kathleen Norris's 2008 book *Acedia and Me* provides a lengthy and historically rich reflection on the difference between depression as a clinical term rooted in the assumptions of psychotherapy and psychiatry and "acedia" as an older term rooted in the discourse of theology and spirituality—the "dryness" often described in spiritual autobiography as a "desert" experience, or, more dramatically, the "dark night of the soul" in which a believer is, for a time, deprived of any lively sense of the presence of God and unable to experience anything redemptive in practices like prayer that are usually sustaining. To be willing to move across the permeable boundary between psychotherapeutic and spiritual paradigms and discourses is potentially to expand and enrich the conversation with patients suffering in the ways Kenyon's poem, as well as Norris's memoir, articulate.

The passing of seasons enumerated in the poem not only reinforces the sense of interminable, relentless ongoingness, but also the dread that arises in the prospect of no end in sight—a feeling encapsulated in the ellipsis that concludes the poem: "Spring comes, summer; / Cool clear weather, heat, rain . . . Inevitability and inescapability are the defining features of the ominous "it." More than the insomnia itself, the loss of appetite, the fatigue, it is the relentless the sense of being stalked or tethered to a malevolent partner presence that focuses the speaker's distress. It even beats her to the door, suggesting there is no hope of outrunning it—a dark, ironic echo of Eliot's line about the omnipresence of the Spirit that "prevents us everywhere."

The spiritual dimension of the depression comes out more explicitly in the mocking question "Where is your God now?"—a classic question as old as the Psalms, as old as the cry of abandonment from the cross, that runs like a thread through the literature of suffering. Especially mental illness raises unavoidable questions about spirituality, since the terms mind and spirit are, for so many, almost contiguous. The sensation of being both trapped and mocked deepens here into a dark night of the soul—an experience not only of attack, but of abandonment.

A poem that provides a similar range of felt experience in response to the inescapable inner "other," though ending in a very different register, is Annie Stenzel's "An Incantation for the Small Hours of the Night." Written shortly after the poet's being diagnosed with multiple sclerosis in 1992, the element of dread dominates the first half of the poem (Stenzel, 290). For the MS patient, the "enemy" is elusive, slow, haunting, and difficult to locate. One can't "point to the place of pain" any more than the person suffering from depression, but must endure the eerie presence both poems describe.

An Incantation for the Small Hours of the Night

Unspeakable some thing is stalking me
silent in its approach

Indifferent some thing has me in its sights
is circling (no malice, just menace)

inexorable, unavoidable

Incomprehensible some thing is there
in the darkness beside me

its presence within sound of my scampering
heartbeat, labored breathing, stifled whimpers

Inescapable some thing has gained entry now

Terror is all I am; my former human
being is usurped. I am the trapped but conscious

animal, the threatened insect, the doomed
(it matters not what kind of) creature

who here awaits one final blow

I live with these unannounced arrivals
of an alien occupant of my mortal form

so Gods, let me bless and cherish every moment
of its absence to arm myself with consciousness

that every earthly darkness has given way to light, thus far.

The poem tracks the development of an apprehension that deepens to a point of complete overwhelm in "Terror is all I am," and then begins the ascent into a place of qualified and reasoned hope. The first six stanzas come in a regular 2-2-1 beat that delivers the speaker's thoughts like irregular heartbeats, each one both a reiteration and an amplification of what came before. They multiply synonyms for what is relentless, inescapable, and mysterious, giving a cumulative effect of mounting anxiety.

Opening the poem with "unspeakable" establishes a paradoxical frame that underscores the ominous vagueness of "thing," which, standing separate from "some" amplifies the ominousness of the presence that can't be named or sighted by the slight hesitation between those two words, so often written as one. As in Kenyon's poem, the pronoun is key: "it," like "thing" emphasizes the impersonal and inhuman character of what oppresses, but the verbs suggest intent that is both malevolent and human. The thing's silence compounds "unspeakable" with unspeaking; the silence is full of portent, but empty of words. In that presence the speaker's words become defenses against a silence that threatens to overwhelm. Some people talk when they're anxious. Words can be woven into shields or into places of shelter. These words provide that, but also lie on the page between the frequent stanza breaks that make the silent "white space" in the poem as conspicuous as the words that bound it.

The second stanza starts in exact parallel rhythm and structure to the first, but introduces a bit of parenthetical reflection that visibly splits the speaker's consciousness into two levels: that which registers and reports feeling, and that which reflects and interprets what is felt. As in the poems discussed earlier, the speaker speaks from two "selves," and the poem sets those different selves in relationship. Here the more discerning, rational, assessing self speaks in parentheses, as though in a whisper, or from behind a protective barrier, clearly subordinated to the self that speaks from anxiety and fear.

"Indifferent" is both human and inhumane. Explaining the attitude of indifference as not malice but menace helps allay a certain kind of fear while simultaneously introducing another: if the "thing" is an inhuman menacing force incapable of malice, one cannot take it on as an actual "enemy," yet precisely because of that it may be less possible to engage the threat in any meaningful way, since no reciprocity is possible. That it is circling evokes a connection with the circling of predatory birds or animals who have spotted their prey. Predation is natural, but brutal, and as such, an apt enough metaphor for a progressive and incurable illness.

To indifference are added "inexorable" and "unavoidable," standing alone, as though the speaker is pausing, searching for a more precise way to get at the nature of the threat. But the hope of such access is stifled in the next word: the thing in the darkness is "incomprehensible." Even its locus is uncertain—beside, within, verging, hovering, merging with the body's own edgy adrenalin-driven reactions to mounting fear. As the fear takes over, the "thing" becomes "inescapable." It has subsumed not only the ambient darkness, but the body itself until the speaker finds her self permeated and transformed by terror. This is the center of the poem—the depth of the pit into which night fears have driven her.

Then begins the ascent. Though the image of a trapped, doomed creature awaiting a death blow hardly seems to signify a return of hope, it does signify a turn of the imagination toward a metaphor that invites identification with all living things that suffer predation and death. The metaphor liberates the speaker from the element of terror that lies in abject isolation. Like the somber ancient words of Qoheleth, "Behold, all flesh is as the grass," there is a paradoxical comfort in the universality of death. "Death comes to us all, my lord," Thomas More is made to say in *A Man for All Seasons*, in calm reply to the threat of execution. So, too, in this poem, the beginning of accepting life on new terms lies in accepting death.

We see that emergence more clearly in the first words of the following stanza: "I live with . . . ." Adaptation to the intermittent exacerbations of MS is beautifully, concisely rendered in the image of "unannounced arrivals / of an alien occupant of my mortal form." The "thing" comes and goes, but the coming and going is not likely to stop, and so one shifts, not into a new but reliable rhythm, a new but manageable set of practices, but into a new level of uncertainty, instability, contingency. This is a particular kind of difficulty, more inchoate than pain or ache or singular loss, and it makes unique spiritual demands.

Aware of the need to arm the spirit for those demands, the speaker ends with a prayer, powerful and moving in its generous, gritty blend of gratitude, trust, and realism. The final phrase, 'thus far," courageously insists that we remember the terms, not only of a life framed by progressive, degenerative illness, but of any life. We live by patterns and promises that are subject to change. We look to what has been to help navigate what will be, but history is an unreliable guide, and memory an unreliable narrator. Still, what we can know and live by can be retrieved and made serviceable by reflection. The hope in this poem lies in the speaker's conviction that consciousness can "arm" her for what is to come, and that the examined life, even when it has become more fragile, painful, and bounded, may yet give way to light.

Patients like these are the "insiders" who offer those of us who remain, for the present, "outside" their far country a map of that place that may enable us to visit them there, accepting their hospitality with the courtesy and diplomacy and reserve their occasions call for. The instructional dimension of their poems lies in their showing us a way, giving us a language, even an etiquette as caregivers—letting us know what is negotiable, what is to be accepted, what is to be contended with, and what, finally, may still be brought to the terms of what Yeats once called "a harder thing than hope."

Chapter Three
Naming the Elephant

I like her. She talks about things. We never talk about things.
—Margaret Dashwood in *Sense and Sensibility*
film script by Emma Thompson

Despite increased clinical candor and much public discussion about illness and disability, some conditions are still spoken of only behind closed doors, or with an edge of unease and an eye on the privacy clause. It has always been the case that some diseases carry a stigma while others invite and receive ready sympathy; the former remain consigned to the shadowy realm of taboo. How to talk about them, even when they are public knowledge, remains emotionally, politically, or theologically complicated. Uncomfortably unmentioned in polite company, such conditions become the unnamed "elephant in the room."

Poets who set themselves the task of writing past that tacit social barrier know their words may give offense. Their disclosures are a kind of "coming out" that locates them in a geography of controversy. Against that backdrop, it may be useful to consider how—and why—three poets take on the risk of stirring up ancient and murky connections between "sin" and sickness, or violating proprieties and codes of privacy to speak about unsavory forms of suffering.

Though it gets so much press as a legal and moral issue, the actual experience of abortion, its physical process and psychological costs, are still less freely discussed than the abstractions in which we more readily clothe it when we discuss it as a theological controversy or legal problem. Even among those who, as a matter of political conviction, support women's right to choose abortion, conversation about personal experiences of abortion can be riddled with emotional pain, ambivalence, guilt, and grief. The loss of something more consequential than blood and tissue is undeniable for the woman who has just traveled the steep trajectory of feeling from lovemaking to pregnancy test to decision-making to clinic. Suddenly she finds herself not only in a new stage of life, but in a new cohort of women who have been through this uniquely difficult and highly charged experience. And it can be as hard for those who are vigorous supporters of the right to choice to admit the complexities and costs of abortion out loud as it is for "pro-life" activists to admit that there may be reasons for it to be kept legally available.

Anne Sexton's poem "The Abortion" faces the physical and psychological facts of loss with bluntness, subtlety, tenderness, and full frontal acknowledgment of trauma, not to mention an odd note of humor that testifies to how life resiliently reasserts itself in the very midst of free-floating sorrow (Sexton, 61). The sorrow itself, though, is pervasive. Everything in the speaker's visual landscape seems to allude to injury and evisceration.

She begins with a deceptively simple and shockingly blunt line that drives to the heart of that loss: "Somebody who should have been born / is gone." Part of the work of mourning enacted here is to move beyond denial to recognizing and accepting the reality and the finality of loss. The poem models that process of "making it real."

The Abortion

Somebody who should have been born
is gone.

Just as the earth puckered its mouth,
each bud puffing out from its knot,
I changed my shoes, and then drove south.

Up past the Blue Mountains, where
Pennsylvania humps on endlessly,
wearing, like a crayoned cat, its green hair,

its roads sunken in like a gray washboard;
where, in truth, the ground cracks evilly,
a dark socket from which the coal has poured,

Somebody who should have been born
is gone.

the grass as bristly and stout as chives,
and me wondering when the ground would break,
and me wondering how anything fragile survives;

up in Pennsylvania, I met a little man,
not Rumpelstiltskin, at all, at all...
he took the fullness that love began.

Returning north, even the sky grew thin
like a high window looking nowhere.
The road was as flat as a sheet of tin.

Somebody who should have been born
is gone.

Yes, woman, such logic will lead
to loss without death. Or say what you meant,
you coward... this baby that I bleed.

The poem circles back three times to its opening cry of lament. One can almost see the speaker behind the wheel, rocking back and forth repeating her mantra of sorrow, narrating her one-sentence story, relocating herself in a world that is now "after."

Another repetition—of images of grass and cracked ground—reinforces the contrast between apparent life and health and the threat of death that seems not specific, but pervasive—as though the abortion is just one manifestation of a much larger force at work to defeat life. This sense that the natural world is somehow participating in one's own sorrows and losses, while a Romantic literary trope, is also an authentic psychological experience; boundaries between inner and outer world blur, in much the same way they do for Hamlet who in his gloom about his father's death and his uncle's betrayal exclaims, "How weary, stale, flat and unprofitable, / Seem to me all the uses of this world! / Fie on't! ah fie! 'tis an unweeded garden, / That grows to seed . . ." (I, ii, 133-136).

With similar literary deftness, the poem's allusion to Rumpelstiltskin, who wove straw into gold, but demanded a woman's firstborn child in return, locates this abortion in the archetypal narrative frame of a desperate victim driven to extreme measures to preserve her own life and well-being, only to learn that what she risks is the life of her unborn child. But in the tale the woman finds a way out: she learns the name of the wicked "little man" who offered her immediate help in return for the forfeiture of her first child, and so wins the cruel bargain and keeps the child. Her cleverness affords her a way out of the appalling loss to which she has agreed. While the fairy-tale identifies the risk or forfeiture of a child as an archetypal predicament (recalling other more ancient tales of sacrifice of the first-born), it also suggests a resolution that this speaker has not been able to find. Some might say, of course, that there is always a way: one can choose to keep a baby or to offer it up for adoption. But this woman's conviction is that what she has done was both necessary and unavoidable. The little man offered no last-minute revelation to spare her. The repetition of "at all," in addition to the accentuated rhythm and rhyme turns the poem into a chant here—a slow four-beat dirge-like recitation of irrecoverable loss, not only of a child, but of the innocence that once allowed her to believe this would not happen to her.

What the little man took was "the fullness that love began"–a phrase with a biblical ring, like "the fullness of time" that both avoids and honors the truth of what was taken and destroyed, sidestepping the vexed theological and political question of whether the fetus is a human being, but not the way this woman experiences this loss—connected to an act of love, a promise unkept, a foreshortening of an unfolding story, a profound disruption in the order of things.

As the speaker drives, she again projects that sense of disruption onto the landscape where they sky grows "thin / like a high window looking nowhere" and the road is "flat as a sheet of tin." "Thin" and "Flat" are descriptors of landscape here, but perhaps ought to be included on the now commonly used lists of diagnostic terms for patients to choose from (pick five of these 50 words for pain, etc.) "Thin" and "flat" are feelings, here projected onto the outer world, just as, earlier, the speaker saw the earth as a projection of her body. Literally what would have made her body round and full has been removed, and she is deflated.

Visual perspective is similarly distorted: the high window looking nowhere reminds one of a Dali painting—a surreal image of radical dislocation, after which she relocates herself with the sad refrain that returns her to the present moment: "Somebody who should have been born is gone" serves as a centering device in the midst of disorientation.

In the final stanza, the speaker takes her own rhetoric to task: all the metaphors, the rhetorical evasions, the abstractions amount to lies if, finally, the literal truth is not uttered: what has happened is a death. It is her body, she is bleeding, and what is being bled is a terminated life. Addressing herself as "woman" is deliberately harsh, though it, too, has a biblical echo in the numerous times Jesus addressed a woman in that way to call her to account; here the speaker is taking herself to task not for the abortion itself, but for her cowardly attempt thus far to mask or mitigate the full truth of what it has entailed. Only facing the bald, literal, physical facts will finally preserve her sense of integrity. The cost of doing this thing, she concludes, is to look at it full on and be willing to grasp its magnitude.

Interestingly, the issue upon which the poem concludes is not the morality of abortion—whether or not it is murder—but the matter of moral courage that is required even of those who have made the decision and carried it through. To admit that what has happened is a real death, that what is lost is a real life, is not necessarily to conclude that it should not have been done, but certainly that to do it exacts an ethical struggle and a psychological cost. The temptation to minimize, explain away, or pretend, and the consequences of doing any of those, the poem suggests, are least as significant a matter for the one who makes the decision as are theoretical arguments about the rightness or wrongness of the decision itself.

Though it is by now the subject of incessant political and religious polemic, abortion remains, in the experience of many women who have considered it, a radically personal decision, entailing, among many others, the question, "Can I live with myself if I do this?" Even among those who support women's right to choose abortion as a matter of political conviction, personal experience of abortion can be riddled with emotional pain, ambivalence, residual guilt, even grief. The loss of something more consequential than blood and tissue is undeniable for the woman who has just traveled the steep trajectory of feeling from lovemaking to pregnancy test to decision making to the clinic. Suddenly she finds herself not only in a new stage of life but in a new cohort of women who have been through this uniquely difficult and highly charged experience.

Another broad cohort that shares insider information seldom discussed among the uninitiated is composed of those who have made the hard and often controversial decision to undergo the rigors and risks of chemotherapy. For some kinds of cancer it seems to many to be the obvious, or only, option for survival. For a range of others, it may be a trickier decision: the treatment can be so harsh and poisonous in some cases that it may seem worse than the disease, if tumors are slow-growing, if the cancer occurs late in life, if the patient's general health might be seriously compromised, or if alternative approaches have shown conspicuous success. In any of these cases, chemo is a matter poorly understood by those who haven't had to sit in an oncologist's office and consider the tradeoffs.

B. A. St. Andrews' wry poem, "Oncological Cocktails" offers an unusual view of chemotherapy by a patient whose plight may be hard and frightening, but who manages to achieve enough critical distance on her treatment to raise some edgy questions about what patients are expected to trust (St. Andrews, 8). Of her professional introduction to the medical world the poet writes, "I had found my strange way home to a place I'd never been before, leaving the illuminating questions of the liberal arts and entering the dubious certainties of medical science. Far from being separate, art and science, I discovered, are Siamese twins joined at the heart. They are two hands clapping (St. Andrews, online)." To the end of her own foreshortened life, poetry was a way of understanding and a way of empathy. She wrote about illness from multiple points of view, including that of the sorrowing oncologist who has lost a patient in "Oncologist Lost"—a helpful and generously imagined complement to "Oncological

Cocktails." St. Andrews wrote about her own work, "Poetry is not enterprising, having no bottom line even in a couplet. It [has] no motive more profitable than articulating the systole and diastole of the heart" (St. Andrews, online).

"Oncological Cocktails" refers specifically to a liquid containing barium that must be drunk before fluoroscopy that determines the extent of cancer growth. The title itself introduces the note of irony that permeates the poem, which likens treatment with cancer drugs to the dubious pleasures of social drinking. The fact that the speaker's first skeptical observation focuses on the youth of the technician and her brisk and presumptuous protocols reinforces the ironic distance between the speaker and the staff who serve her.

Oncological Cocktails

Looking too young to barkeep
the technician comes in shaking
a beaker that froths and hisses

like volcanic vodka or a martini
prepared by Dr. Hyde. Artless
as an egg she offers me

this cocktail neat or on
the rocks and won't take
no for an answer. We

do not speak of cancer.
This barium refresher is
ninety proof and guaranteed

to knock me sober. Served
with a twist it tastes
and smells like a nuclear waste

site laced with a splash of lye.
Trying to be as philosophical
as a Greek and brave as a Roman

gladiator I quaff this pewter
sludge without flinching,
without betraying my mortal

fear the fluoroscopy will
show my troops have
broken rank and an enemy

army of metastasizing cells
is advancing, armed and dangerous,
along my exposed flank.

Have I already lost a battle
or two against these
brash aggressors who sail

their warships like pleasure
boats up my defenseless
coast to set up camp along

my shores? Accepting that
I must join forces with
allies I neither know nor

trust I lift your proffered
cup as Socrates must
have, one eye on the door.

If the technician is too young to barkeep, she is surely too young to do this. The opening phrase establishes the wry tone that carries us through a series of observations and allusions that reframe the unpleasant treatment in large, fanciful terms that confer upon it the dignities of heroic battle and Socratic wisdom as well as the tolerant perspective of a veteran of as dubious a process as war or political contest. Colleagues writing about the poet comment, "She learned about medicine's tools—sonograms, chemotherapy, the scalpel—with a mixture of curiosity and skepticism"—an ambivalence that gives this poem its dimension and depth.

The simile in the second stanza linking the young technician to an egg is curiously suggestive: she is still in the early stages of her own development. There is a provocative innocence in her stubborn, unquestioning, dutiful routine. Under her white coat she is all potential, performing the all-too-unconscious acts of a trainee with the meticulous evasiveness that passes for professionalism. The irony, of course, is compounded by the commonplace observation that people too young to drink legally in this culture are routinely provided with uniforms and guns and authorized to kill. She's "only" a technician, not, presumably, someone who thoroughly understands the consequences of her work. Like a slightly pushy cocktail waitress, she has the patient in an environment where "just saying no" is neither easy nor appropriate. But her "offer," of course, is a requirement. The speaker's impulse to resist is moot, under the circumstances, so they play out a social ritual of polite offer and free acceptance, though in fact the exchange is fraught with multiple tensions of the sort Gilda Radner described far more forthrightly in her cancer narrative, *It's Always Something*:

> I had a chip on my shoulder—and a lump in my throat. I cried through the whole setup. The technicians marked my body front and back with small dots to line me up for a thirty-second radiation treatment—like a long X-ray—on an area from below my breasts to my crotch on the front, and the equivalent on the back. I hated everyone: the technicians, the radiologist, the nurses, even the physicists who made the blocks that protected my vital organs from the radiation treatment. (Radner, 205)

To be utterly dependent on those who are hurting you in ways and at levels you've not had to imagine is an insult that has little to do with rational understanding of therapeutic measures that mask their kindness in cruelty.

So acquired dread and inner resistance masquerading as acquiescence become part of the pre-treatment rituals. And then there is the treatment, itself. The frank melodrama of a frothing and hissing liquid potion mentioned in the poem links the young technician to the mad scientists of Victorian literature and to wizards and mages of legend and lore, making her complicit in a Faustian plot to which neither she nor the patient is entirely privy. Few technicians and fewer patients carry into their daily regimens the larger questions that deserve to be raised about the pharmaceutical industry, the toxicity of postindustrial life, the relationships between the poisons we suffer from and the poisons we look to for healing. That the 90-proof "barium refresher" tastes "like a nuclear waste site laced with a splash of lye," and that the speaker "quaffs" as Socrates did the hemlock acknowledges fully and shockingly the troubling paradox of chemotherapy and links it to the many other ways we create and accept death-dealing substances in the interests of maintaining the lives we've devised and called normal. The doubled-edged character of Jekyll and Hyde—the one a man of honest curiosity and scientific integrity, the other a power-mad experimenter who justifies lethal exploitation of others in the interests of his single-minded obsessions—provides an allusion worth the uncomfortable exploration it invites, such as that undertaken by Ralph W. Moss in *The Cancer Industry*, where he writes,

> If cancer specialists were to admit publicly that chemotherapy is of limited usefulness and is often dangerous, the public might demand a radical change in direction—possibly toward unorthodox and non-toxic methods, and toward cancer prevention. ...The use of chemotherapy is even advocated by those members of the establishment who realize how ineffective and dangerous it can be. (Moss, 84)

This, of course, is the unnamed "elephant" in the oncology treatment center, and in the poem. Though it plays at the edges of the hard questions, the poet leaves it to the reader to consider just how questionable now common treatment practices in fact are.

That the patient and his technician "do not speak of cancer" is another reminder of how much is hidden in the process of treatment not only by dint of institutional protocols and marketing devices, but by a tacit diplomacy that obscures and forestalls the hard questions. The social contract peculiar to this site of treatment is predicated on largely unquestioning submission—obeying orders like the soldier who "must join forces with allies" they "neither know nor trust." Several stanzas develop the metaphor so common, especially in oncology, of the patient as fighter and the body as a site of battle. Like a foot-soldier, the patient is kept in a certain ignorance of the plans and strategies upon which her life depends. But still, like Socrates, she keeps "one eye on the door," considering escape even as she drinks down the toxic compounds.

Beyond a darkly amusing representation of a patient's reluctance to undergo the nausea, malaise, deep fatigue and physical debility that generally accompany chemotherapy, the poem obliquely takes on the problem of chemotherapy as a way of healing made possible, and perhaps necessary, by a culture in which such high levels of toxicity are tolerated to the point of becoming normal, "acceptable," and even normative: nuclear waste, pesticides, exhaust fumes, factory farm runoff, plastic nurdles in the bellies of marine mammals and in the food chain. The patient's misgivings deserve a hearing: is this what healing looks like? Are our sicknesses really so different from the practices we presume belong to abundant and healthy living? The metastasizing cells may be the "aggressors," but their point of invasion is the "defenseless coast," the "shores," the "exposed flank" where the body meets the world, the ambient air and water, the fumes, the UV rays, the irradiated soil. To speak of this illness solely in terms of individual physiology is to miss the essential fact that it is a function of a complex social contract in which we all participate, following orders, perhaps, a little too compliantly, quaffing our colas and cabernets without much question about the cumulative costs of chemical byproducts and questionable farming methods. Every cancer case deserves to be scrutinized through the lens this poet holds up, daring us to see what we see when we peer through it into and beyond the oncology treatment center.

The theme of insidious institutional control over the terms of treatment also emerges provocatively in Patricia Goedicke's "In the Hospital," most recently published in a collection of poems by women on breast cancer (Goedicke, 2). It is one of many of her poems that deal with illness and come out of years of her doing just that. In a commentary on Goedicke's final book of poems, published after her death of lung cancer in 2006, Ron Slate writes of meeting her in 1982, several years into Goedicke's struggle with breast cancer:

> Her mother had died of breast cancer twelve years earlier; her father had lung cancer and multiple sclerosis. In her poetry, beginning with *Between Oceans* (Harcourt, 1968) and continuing through twelve books, her fixation on frailty was both an ambush and an embrace. The sheer physicality of her materials, the bodily presences, inspire summaries of her work that catalog her carnal subjects and emotional extremes. When Patricia died in 2006 of cancer, the obituaries noted how her poems dealt with her illnesses, the love of her husband, and the reality of death. (Slate, online)

The "sheer physicality" Slate mentions is evident in "In the Hospital," as well as a careful record of the emotional fluctuations associated with treatment. In eight cryptic couplets she records a succession of submissions to increasingly invasive procedures, admitting both her complicity and a certain willful ignorance toward the process.

In the Hospital

When they came at me with sharp knives
I put perfume under my nose,

When they knocked me out on the operating table
I dreamed I was flying

When they asked me embarrassing questions
I remembered the clouds in the sky,

When they were about to drown me
I floated

On their inquisitive glances I drifted
like a leaf becalmed in a pool.

When they laid harsh hands on me
I thought of fireworks I had seen with you,

When they told me I was sick and might die
I left them and went away with you to where I live,

When they took off my right breast
I gave it to them.

The anonymity of the "they" in question here conveys an impression of medical personnel who are impersonal, aggressive, intrusive, insensitive, and demanding. The succession of invasive procedures the speaker has undergone are represented as forms of torture, and her coping methods as increasingly strenuous strategies of avoidance—distraction, fantasy, meditation, memory—until at last she "gives" her breast to those who take it. In a series of active sentences that follow a fatalistic pattern of repetition, she presents herself both as agent and as victim. The "I" who is the subject of each sentence both participated in and resisted treatment until the final act of submission that comes as a tragic capitulation at the end after the tension has been held for seven grim couplets.

The couplet form works to particular purpose in this poem, signifying the agon enacted between physicians and patient—an argument consisting of authorized procedures on their part and passive resistance on hers. Each couplet arrives at its own closure, as though the dreadful march toward mastectomy might be halted there—as though each desperate attempt to forestall the increasingly inevitable decision offers its own renewal of faint hope. The couplets also, of course, emphasize the "twoness" or natural pairing of the body's symmetries about to be destroyed. The sense of ritual sacrifice in the final "I gave it to them" suggests an offering to an imperious deity who will only be satisfied with a costly offering of blood and flesh.

The abusive character of "their" approaches raises a similar—and similarly oblique—question to that implied in Andrews' poem above: is this the only way? Is there a way out? Must healing look like this? Some would say no: international comparisons of breast cancer survival rates suggest that there are viable alternatives to radical mastectomy and that perhaps the American tendency to rush to surgery needs to be reexamined (see Payer, Ch. 4). Certainly this poem asks readers to consider the cost of the surgical option in psychological terms, but it is not the poem of an activist; few in the throes of treatment feel they can afford to challenge the system from which they seek help, and so even the skeptical often remain ambivalent.

The speaker's psychological state is thus articulated in the pregnant succession of images that depict her response to each incursion. Meeting the "sharp knives" with perfume under her nose seems pathetically irrelevant and ineffectual, but also recalls the classic Victorian woman who protects her delicate self from the olfactory insults of urban squalor with perfume and is revived from the fainting spells believed to be a mark of femininity by smelling salts. Her first line of defense, in other words, against this assault on a primary sign of womanhood is to reassert her femininity with a prototypically feminine gesture. Her second line of defense comes in another classic image—the flying dream, widely interpreted as an image of personal power. Knocking her out sends her to the refuge of the unconscious in which she recognizes a psychological resource that, tragically, fails to change her fate in waking life. In response to humiliation she remembers "clouds in the sky," seeking peace in the open, cosmic space of reverie, perhaps even in a fantasy of disembodiment, spiritualizing the moment to avoid its pain. Floating when "they" were about to drown her indicates another ingeniously passive response to overwhelm—to ride the waves of agony as women in labor are often advised to stay on top of the pain of contractions. Drifting like a leaf in a pool betokens a similar assumed indifference to buffetings, emphasized by the fact that as a drifting leaf she imagines herself "becalmed"—directionless, still, and inert, like an animal frozen to protect itself against the predator's roving eye.

The tension rises in the sixth couplet when "they laid harsh hands" on her. Her response is to remember the fireworks seen with the "you" to whom the poem is suddenly and directly addressed. Becoming so belatedly a dialogue also changes the terms of what has up until then seemed an internal act of remembering. Now we see that the plea is being made to an other who might rescue her, but hasn't. The fireworks suggest the explosiveness of the emotion being suppressed in the long process of enduring a desecration against which she can't defend herself or, apparently, be defended by friend or lover. The penultimate stanza, and strategy, is to resort to complete retreat—the "I want to go home" of the homesick child. The simplicity of the wish to go home is also archetypal—where the speaker "lives" is not here, but elsewhere: what she experiences here she cannot identify as life.

But in the last lines, when the breast is finally taken, the poignancy of all her efforts comes to a sad and dignified climax: she reclaims her dignity, her body, and even a kind of priestly authority, in fully claiming responsibility for the amputation as a giving and the severed breast as a gift.

The words of the poem come from a retrospective vantage point: the speaker is one who has undergone all these horrors and survived—not without bitterness, but also without final humiliation and defeat. This remarkable poem traces a psychological journey from terror to avoidance to resistance to capitulation to reclamation of self in a way that allows full room for the perspective of a patient who, though she may be cured by the stratagems of aggressive surgery, gives herself permission not to glorify the process, but to see it as the horror that it is. Perhaps the cure is not worse than the disease, but it may in its way be as fearsome.

Chapter Four
Outrageous Intimacies

*Put your feet in these stirrups. Okay. Just. There. Okay? Now. Oh, I have
to go get Susie. Got to have a girl in here. Some crazy clinical rule. Um. I'll
be right back. Don't move.*
— Jason Posner in *Wit* by Margaret Edson

I recall a young male doctor's observation that one of the more difficult aspects
of family medicine was to "meet a woman your mother's age, chat with her
for less than five minutes, and then tell her to undress." The breaches of social
decorum that are allowed, acceptable, and even routine in medicine remain,
especially for patients, transgressive—and not only patients, but professional
caregivers have often to wrestle with the fluctuating notions of decorum that
allow them access to others' bodies and extremely personal histories. An article
on "professional etiquette" in the *British Medical Journal* in 1871 pronounces
firmly and clearly, "[It is] our duty to indicate . . . the necessity of permitting
no relaxation in the strictness of a rule of public modesty which is important
to the character of our profession and to the public interests (*BMJ*, 760)." Such
certainties seem quaint, if not amusing, now; modesty itself is a sliding scale
in a multicultural environment—a fact corroborated by the number of articles
on patient concerns about privacy and modesty that focus on clinical encoun-
ters with particular ethnic or immigrant groups. Especially, but not only, when
crossing gender lines to touch, examine, and inquire about the most intimate
parts of patients' bodies and lives, doctors and other caregivers may struggle,
like the young physician quoted above, with their own discomforts about the
changed terms of social contact in clinical settings, but may not always be fully
aware of what it costs the patient to consent to such invasions. Moreover, a
self-protective impulse deeper than social decorum makes many women hesi-
tate, stiffen, or recoil, at least inwardly, when subjected even to the most legiti-

mate clinical exposure, and may leave them with a distressing sense of having been violated, however appropriate the contact and important the information gained.

Alice Jones' "The Biopsy" chronicles a patient's experience of such a permitted invasion, during which the male doctor appears to remain curiously unconscious of the discomfort even of a woman who has decided to watch her own breast being prepared, cut, and biopsied (Jones, 43-44).

The Biopsy

The dapper surgeon enters, greets me
loudly, hangs his coat on a steel hook
next to my slip, as in a cozy household.
I lie down and we begin. He preps
with those large orange Q-tips—
betadine swabs—poking objectively,
then asks for lidocaine and fussily
tells the nurse to wipe the top
of the unopened bottle with alcohol.
The fine needle stings, bites deeper.
He arranges the green cloth drape,
the last has an open square at its center,
so my now-orange nipple protrudes through,
one spot of nakedness among our hospital gowns,
an absurd striptease. Now the silver
dish-lights are focused on this point,
the small flesh star, from which
the whole scene radiates. He calls
for a #15 blade, which then glides
without pain, just a pull.
I had thought my skin was a permanent seal.
Now I watch this layer of myself,

this pale field, sprout red flowers
in a sudden watercoloring,
as the scalpel makes its first nick,
then the dark trail blooms, spills over.
A wet trickle crosses my ribs,
and he asks for the cautery.
It crackles, clotting off small vessels,
making a tasty smell of fat,
like chicken skin frying. He sets
the handle down on the drape
half across my face. Caught
in the rhythm of his concentrated
breathing, I close my eyes, hear
the metallic nips of his scissors,
feel the quick daubs of gauze.
Trying to be elsewhere,
I think of the morning paper,
but only remember the photographs—
the planetary curve of Neptune,
the shadow of its Great Dark Spot.
When he calls for the chromic, I know
I'm now being repaired. I glance down
to find my nipple being lifted
off to the right, grasped by
the stainless-steel teeth of the forceps,
beside a meaty red hole, empty now,
its small harvest reaped. I picture
the journey of the dense, yellow marble
with blood-tinged edges, this aborted
piece of me, traveling to the lab
in a clear bottle of formalin,
where they'll set it in wax,
layer it by microtome, then examine

each section, my cellular patterns.
Suturing the red place, he asks
how I'm doing, his first words.
I gaze at him, his all-white hair,
his smile as he says that the nodule
will prove benign, this man
who went beyond my skin
as no one else has, to see my body
opened by his working hands
as he made me for the first time, his.

The poem begins in recoil: "dapper" and "fussy" suggest the speaker's immediate critical reaction to the surgeon's behavior and dress that so distinctly differentiate him from the gowned and waiting patient. He "pokes objectively," without much attention to her exposure, the enforced intimacy of the situation, the unsettling irony involved in his hanging his coat next to her slip. For the woman the whole process is alienating. The necessary violation of privacy is carried out with what passes for appropriate clinical detachment, but what she experiences as distastefully businesslike.

The verbs describing the surgeon's meticulous preparations—he greets, preps, pokes, arranges, calls for, asks, and finally "makes me"—suggest order, ritual, and control. The procedure is prescribed and carried out with matter-of-fact precision. He knows what he's doing—in a certain sense. In another, he seems to have no clue. The verbs that describe what is happening from the patient's point of view have a very different feel. Her nipple "protrudes." The scene "radiates" from the "small flesh star," one point on her body. The blade "pulls" on her skin, which "sprouts" the red flowers of blood after the incision. The cautery "crackles" like frying chicken fat. The scissors make their nips, and the tissue is "reaped" like a "small harvest." And she "imagines" the journey of that sample to the lab, the slicing, the peering, the staining that will provide the information the doctor is after. Her body is a site, a scene, a piece of meat, a piece of earth, her skin a barrier to be broken. There is a courageous precision as well as invention in the images and analogies the poet appropriates to articulate the process from her point of view as someone upon whom this invasive procedure is being performed, who has to find a way to accept what she, like all of us, is deeply conditioned to protect herself from—the exposure, the touching, the cutting, the marring.

She had thought her skin "was a permanent seal." This line adds disillusionment to the succession of experiences recorded. The protective barrier we are born with will not protect us. We find this out with our first cut or skinned knee, and discover it again in the shock of blood, every time. The slightly surreal vision of her body as a field sprouting flowers, then as a canvas being painted provides a view from beneath or below of mysterious, gradual disclosures. Despite anxiety and discomfort, cutting the body evokes fascination.

Among the images are words that signify informed familiarity with the tools and procedures of surgery—the cautery that clots off small vessels, the chromic, the forceps, the formalin, the microtome. This is no ordinary patient, but a trained physician, willing to witness her own surgery, and one capable of the bifocal vision required to observe clinically while also making detailed and respectful note of her deeply subjective responses, like a speaker doing her own simultaneous translation.

Some of the language is jarring: "tasty" like "striptease" or "meaty red hole" is vaguely offensive, slightly comic, certainly irreverent, as though one strategy of self-protection in this arduous witnessing is the imaginative play we see in the poem. That playfulness is slightly bawdy, as though any penetration of the body—especially of an erotically sensitive area—has unavoidably sexual overtones.

Her effort "to be elsewhere" seems to lead her to another image: the picture of Neptune in the morning paper with its curve and its dark spot serve to mirror her own body with its suspicious spot. Like dream material, a picture of a planet becomes a figure of the self that emphasizes the awesome remoteness and mystery of the body whose most potent processes are hidden from the conscious mind. Many illness narratives and poems have this element of projection in common: bodily suffering colors the way one sees the world. The so-called "pathetic fallacy" developed deliberately in Romantic poetry—by which feelings are ascribed to the nonhuman world, a grey day is melancholy, a babbling brook is playful, etc.—is not just a literary device, but a habit of mind to which one is particularly prone when the intimate habitat of the body is disrupted.

The poet's attention returns abruptly from her cosmic dream moment to the jarring sight her nipple being lifted by the "stainless steel teeth of the forceps." She reports this process in with alarming matter-of-factness, though the "teeth" that leave a "meaty red hole" represent the instrument as predator and her body as prey. Another highly charged word, "aborted," forges a similar link between this procedure and another that, however quick and clinical, is inescapably distressing and repugnant.

Professional knowledge of what technicians will do to her tissue sample in the lab is cold comfort. It is not at all clear that there is reassurance in this knowledge. Indeed, the phrase "this piece of me" cancels the apparent objectivity of pathology protocols. Though the technicians may be looking at a tissue sample, she cannot and will not consent to regarding any piece of personal flesh as neutral matter.

The final ambiguity of the poem lies in its allusion to the themes of power and sexuality: the physician has made her "his" by entering her body; he has done this thing with her consent, to be sure, but has gained the information needed by taking something from her that leaves her scarred and changed. That it was worth the cost is not directly questioned, but that the cost is considerable and deeply personal is the primary message of the poem—that it is good not to underestimate the tradeoffs in which medical technologies involve us.

We see a similar reflection on the enforced intimacies of diagnosis and surgery in a series of eight poems by Chana Bloch, collectively entitled "In the Land of the Body," that chronicle her diagnosis and treatment for ovarian cancer (Bloch, 68). The poems, by a poet and writer whose diagnosis interrupted a thriving teaching career, were composed in the course of treatment, the first scribbled in the car immediately after learning she would have to have surgery. That was her moment of resolve to survive and write about it; that resolve, she said later in an interview, "would be like a thread I could hold on to." She continued to write her way through the experience, jotting notes during clinical visits, collecting unfamiliar words, pressing the doctor for explanations she later translated into her own idiom. Thus, in the second of the poems, an ordinary clinical conversation about her X-rays is recalled as a confrontation with an eerily schematic representation of her own body and a doctor whose authority merges the roles of fortune-teller, scientist, and teacher, though in a later those roles morph into that of an intimate other, unnervingly like a lover.

> He shows me my body translated
> into swirls of light on a fluorescent screen.
>
> This is the thorax with its curving
> fingers of rib, its thick
> ring of fat. These
> are the soft blind organs, huddled, the lungs
> filled with black air.
> This is a transverse section
> of the spinal column: a white eye,
> a dark pupil.
>
> I'm waiting for him to read
> my fortune:
> values on a scale, relative
> shades of gray.
>
> Inside me everything's in color, glossy,
> opaque. A lump of pain
> in a hidden pocket.
>
> His voice segmented, exact, he
> talks to the picture,
> takes a crayon, draws
> a burst of rays
> around the star he's discovered
> but hasn't named.

Subtly here, more overtly in a few of the other poems, the sexual dimension of this intimate encounter between a male doctor working from a place of professional empowerment and a female patient, disempowered, or at least out of her element, is suggested: "He shows me my body." As a lover may also do, the doctor reveals to a woman her own body in a way she could not know it on her own.

Subtly, too, the poem recalls the famous consultation with Madame Sosostris, "famous clairvoyante" in *The Waste Land*, a quasi-comic figure who dispenses reassurance or satisfies the curiosity of the gullible by playing out a ritual whose potency lies in the need that drives the seeker to believe that what she can tell him will save him. The doctor's "This is the thorax . . . / These are the soft, blind organs . . . / This is a transverse section" picks up the portentious rhythms of the clairvoyante's words: "Here is Belladonna, the Lady of the Rocks / . . . Here is the man with three staves . . . / Here is the one-eyed merchant, and this card, / Which is blank, is something he carries on his back, / Which I am forbidden to see" (Eliot, WL, 31).

Waiting for the fortuneteller's prediction one wrestles with indecision about what to allow oneself—or force oneself—to believe. Like the clairvoyante who utters the names of the cards, the doctor is performing a rite of initiation, pointing to the hidden parts patient's body, readable only to the trained eye, identifying, mapping, verifying his diagnosis and thus his authority to enter this body, no longer a sacred space cloistered in protective flesh, but exposed, reduced and estranged, on an impersonal screen.

This poem, the second in the series, was composed of notes taken as the poet looked at that screen and followed the doctor's moving crayon along the map of her own undiscovered country. Some of the lines are lifted directly from her notes—"found poetry," as some poets call it—disclosed in the most ordinary or here, clinical, language. She drew pictures, diagrams, that resembled what she saw: a white eye with a dark pupil, organs in imagined colors, a "picket of ribs." The drawings gave her words. In an interview she explained that a later poem began in the doctor's answer to her question, "What did the tumor look like?" Lobular, membranous, hemorrhagic. She wrote a poem about the tumor that "originally had all those words in it," but later she took them out;

they "limited the poem too much." The doctor sat with her for an hour some months after the operation, reviewing her X-rays. "Some of the words in these poems are his words," she said. The poems grew out of the attempt to speak a foreign language in a foreign land, finding even familiar objects and expressions detached from their accustomed meanings. She entered this conversation with voracious curiosity, informed, she said, by trauma and relief.

A very different kind of unsettling intimacy comes with organ donation and implantation, a procedure that often challenges a patient's basic feelings (as well as those of the donor or donor's family) about the integrity of the body and its identification with self. In an article about "pitfalls in emotionally related organ donation," Nikola Biller-Andorno and Henning Schauenburg reflect on several cases that represent a range of problems live donation can raise among family members who struggle with deep ambivalences about putting oneself or one's loved one at such risk. These problems include the likelihood that the potential donor will feel unduly pressured by other family members; the psychological aftermath for either donor or recipient, including significant change in a relationship that has involved intimate mutuality; and ambiguous motivations masquerading as altruism (Biller-Andorno, 162-4).

Their discussion and others indicate observable differences in attitude among ethnic groups with regard to live organ donation to family members. Recognizing the complexities of the decision, even when it may seem entirely voluntary, open-hearted, and necessary, helps to contextualize Lucille Clifton's gutsy poem, "donor," addressed to the daughter who donated a kidney to keep her alive (Clifton, 17). As many recipients have testified, receiving an organ from a live donor creates a strange new relationship unlike any other; receiving one from someone known and loved radically revises a shared story. In Clifton's case, that story began darkly, in light of which the gift of her daughter's kidney brings about a surprising and generous, but ironic resolution.

donor

to lex

when they tell me that my body
might reject
i think of thirty years ago
and the hangers i shoved inside
hard trying not to have you.
i think of the pills, the everything
i gathered against your
inconvenient bulge; and you
my stubborn baby child,
hunched there in the dark
refusing my refusal.
suppose my body does say no
to yours. again, again i feel you
buckled in despite me, lex,
fastened to life like the frown
on an angel's brow.

The extraordinary honesty of this poem is breathtaking. Addressed to the daughter who donated her kidney, Clifton begins with a bald confession of the efforts she made to abort when she was pregnant with her. Many parents might well and understandably choose not to disclose such hard-edged truths to a child who survived the fear and resistance to a sixth pregnancy. And to make such a confession public takes another kind of audacity.

Ending the first line with "my body" makes a subtle but important distinction between the woman who exercises choice and the body that has its own intelligence and will. Leaving no object after "rejects" makes a transitive verb oddly intransitive, as though the rejection has nothing to do with what is being rejected, but is a disposition of the body itself, so that a distance is established between act and attitude or intention.

The painful image of hangers shoved inside, however, is radically intentional, and is compounded by the explicit explanatory phrase that follows—"trying not to have you." One wonders, of course, what it might be like to be on the receiving end of such blunt honesty. But when we reach the line, "my stubborn baby child" we see how the poem transcends the speaker's residual shame in her admiration for the child's tenacity, her will to live then and, by extension, her will to keep her mother alive now. The mother seems to draw her own life force now from the daughter she names tenderly in the final stanza. "Fastened to life" is not only a long-established fact of survival, but a quality of character that the mother counts on in her dependency on the daughter's gift of life.

The poem represents a complex range of conflicting emotions on the part of the speaker as she faces transplant surgery: a sense of deep irony, a sense of the pathos of her own desperate situation 30 years previously—she neither excuses her abortion attempt nor apologizes for it—amazed appreciation for the gift her daughter gives and the gift she is, even a trace of humor in the final image of her "fastened to life like the frown / on an angel's brow." Though she is fully aware of her own present need as she faces the very real possibility of her own death, she faces it with a lively sense of the wild possibilities that overturn desperate plans.

In a radio interview with Grace Cavalieri, Clifton explained, "This is a poem written to my youngest daughter when I had a kidney transplant. She donated her kidney to me, and what I think is interesting is this: I had six children in six and a half years, and she was the youngest, and she was the child I tried...I did quite a number of things to not have her, which she knows very well; I don't keep things like secrets from my children. And I did things that I say are still illegal. But, she was bound and determined to be born. . . . She said to me that if she had been able to talk, she would have said, "Give me thirty years, and you're gonna need me!" (Clifton, online).

The mother's kidney failure has actualized that need and brought about a depth of connection neither could have anticipated.

Unanticipated intimacies of a very different sort can arise among those who find themselves sharing the exposed spaces of the hospital, and disturb patients into uneasy reflection on how thin are the partitions that keep us separate and protected from others' pain. In "Recovery Room" William Matthews recalls the disoriented hours he spent in the company of strangers as the beginning of a longer journey than he would have expected, and not yet completed (Matthews, 184). Lying among other post-anaesthesia patients, he and they in liminal states of consciousness as they gradually awaken, he finds himself connected to them in ways he could not have predicted.

Recovery Room

How bright it would be, I'd been warned.
To my left an old woman keened steadily,
help me, help me, and steadily a nurse delivered
false and stark balm to her crumpled ear:
You'll be all right. Freshly filleted, we lay

drug-docile on our rolling trays, each boat
becalmed in its slip. I was numb waist-down
to wherever I left off, somewhere between my waist
and Budapest, for I was pointed feet-first east.
I had the responsibility of legs, like tubes

of wet sand, but no sensation from them.
Anyone proud of his brain should try to drag
his body with it before bragging. I had to wait
for my legs and bowels and groin to burn
not with their usual restlessness but

back toward it from anaesthetic null. I felt—
if feel is the right verb here—like a diver
serving time against the bends. And O

there were eight of us parked parallel
as piano keys against the west wall of that
light-shrill room, and by noon we were seven,
though it took me until I got to the surface
to miss her. Especially if half of me's been trans-
planted by Dr. Flowers, the anesthesiologist,
I'm divided, forgetful. I hated having an equator,

below which my numb bowels stalled and my bladder
dully brimmed. A terrible remedy for these
drug-triggered truancies was "introduced,"
as the night nurse nicely put it, and all
the amber night I seeped into a plastic pouch,

and by dawn, so eager was I to escape, and ever
the good student, I coaxed my bowels to turn
a paltry dowel. Here was proof for all of us:
my legs were mine to flee on once again.
Even a poet can't tell you how death enters

an ear, but an old woman whose grating voice
I hated and whose pain I feared died next to me
while I waited like a lizard for the first fizzles
of sensation from my lower, absent, better half:
and like a truculent champagne,

the bottom of my body loosed a few
petulant bubbles, then a few more,
and then. . . . You know the rest.
Soon they let me go home and I did.
Welcome back, somebody said. Back? Back?

The edgy, rueful humor of this poem works in counterpoint to its subtle acknowledgement of loss and even mourning. The woman next to the speaker in the recovery room—at first merely a source of irritation with her steady keening and the platitudinous words of comfort it elicits from the nurse—does not recover. To have lain near her in her last moments disturbs and sobers him, though it doesn't take away his wish to escape, or the wry humor that leads him to imagine himself and the others in a wild succession of metaphors as fish, "freshly filleted," laid out for further processing, then as boats "becalmed" in their slips, then as a sand sculpture, a diver, a mute piano key, a plant, a lizard. The implied logic of these metaphors—macabre, poignant, amusing—sets up crosscurrents of energy that deepen the complexity of the emotional state the poem articulates. He feels exposed, divided, muted, paralyzed. Though the speaker does recover, it is with a sense of having been through a shift of perspective that challenges the commonplace notion of recovery as return to where one started. One does not, the poem insists, emerge from surgery or hospitalization unchanged.

The poem's humor persists in the carnival-mirror dimensions of the body with its "equator" leaving off "somewhere between my waist and Budapest," and in the "paltry dowel" and "petulant bubbles" emerging "like truculent champagne" from reinvigorated bowels—the clinical becomes slightly scatological as normality returns, and with it the social constraints pertaining to bodily functions.

The question with which the poem ends critiques the oversimplified idea of recovery as return, and invites us to consider how illness and hospitalization leave people at a new vantage point, even if they emerge competent to take up their lives again. They take them up from a new place, a new awareness of mortality, a new relationship to the vulnerable and aging body and, surprisingly, a new citizenship in what Susan Sontag called "the kingdom of the sick" (Sontag, 3). This speaker has met a fellow traveler in that kingdom, and, remembering her, the constellation of relationships that define him has been reconfigured.

All these poems testify to the fact that illness involves exposure, thinning of social boundaries, sometimes loss of psychological shields. What it opens people to can be surprisingly healing, or can amplify physical suffering with shame and confusion. The difference between those effects often lies with the caregivers—how they navigate the diplomatic challenges of the clinical setting, how they enact the courtesies that enable patients to tolerate the "transgressions" of invasive procedures, how they communicate compassion even from a "clinical distance." Certainly such compassion requires a lively awareness of how what have become routine procedures to the practitioner may be threatening or shaming or unnerving to patients who, when they walk or are wheeled through the double doors of a hospital, find themselves very far from home.

Chapter Five
The Fear Factor

When I have fears that I may cease to be
Before my pen has glean'd my teeming brain . . .
—John Keats

The fears that accompany illness are not always easy to name. Fear of death, fear of pain, fear of loss of function or identity are obvious byproducts of certain kinds of suffering, but even those may show up in odd and surprising ways and times. Patients' poems map those landscapes of fear, marking out their extent and boundaries, their hidden places and broad blistering plains. Sometimes the fear is straightforward and literal: one is afraid of a slow, painful going, afraid his loved ones will not stay the course of her illness, afraid the work she loves will be consigned to someone else. Sometimes fear feels more inchoate and dreamlike, like a looming encounter with a threatening other. Personifying it sometimes conveys a sense of being stalked, watched, haunted, awaited. Other times fear is a free-floating apprehension expressed only in a succession of suggestive metaphors that offer "ways of putting it."

Fear of foreseeable suffering requires a decision: name it or deny it; walk through it or look for ways around it; resist it or accept it. To say "I am afraid," may open up new avenues of self-knowledge, and even enable a certain relaxation from the rigors of doing battle. Beverlye Hyman-Fead's poem "Vulnerable" articulates an inner dialogue between the courageous and the fearful self, allowing them equally plausible and permissible points of view (Fead, unpub.). Written in hospice after the poet was given two months to live, the dread may be more clearly focused than the unspecified anxiety of the recently diagnosed whose chances of survival are much less clearly proscribed. A painter by vocation, she found that she simply couldn't paint after receiving her diagnosis, but, needing "somewhere to put my feelings" found her way to a poetry workshop that became a place to work through the fear—work that eventuated in two books in the course of a much longer survival than anticipated (the poet is still quite alive and writing).

Vulnerable

What is it you're frightened of?
asks my warrior side.
What fills your heart with such dread?
What happened to your coat of bravery you wore so confidently?
I feel like a deer sometimes, I answer.
I'm not always like you.
I want to lie down in flower-kissed pastures,
let my eyes close against the sun.
I don't want to be poised for battle, I say.
My buttons can't always cover what's inside.
Don't be disappointed with what you see, I plead.
More kindly now, my warrior side asks,
But what is it you are really frightened of?
The possibilities of the inevitable,
I manage to say in my soft deer voice.

The "warrior's" questions that initiate this conversation neither mock nor shame the frightened, deer-like self, but seem posed in authentic curiosity: if you have the capacity to live bravely with the hard facts you have to face, why would you lay down your sword and shield and give way to fear? And why would you make a space for it in the heart that is capable of courage?

The voice of the self that feels fear answers with an image: I feel like a deer. Deer are not simply fearful, but watchful and quick to protect themselves in graceful flight. Between those flights they rest quietly and beautifully in lush and comforting places. They eat, they graze, though not like sheep with a shepherd, but wild and unprotected except by the edge of healthy fear that is their protection against the predators that hedge their repose and keep their sleep light. The image is rich with implication. It is not abject, but suggests a certain beauty and dignity in the person who knows the extent of her own vulnerability, fully feels it, and is able to admit to the rational fear it evokes.

Many patients have taken issue with the common encouragement to "fight," to do battle against cancer, even to rage against the dying of the light. Anne Hawkins writes of a pacifist who urged his oncologist to give up that language entirely, as he had no inclination to be a fighter, and found it not only unhelpful, but counterproductive. He explains, "I knew my health would not come as a result of fighting my illness, but rather as a by-product of seeking my connection to the power within me. . . . The virus was not really the enemy. There was no enemy without. . . . He who wields force is weak" (Hawkins, 71).

In "Vulnerable" the speaker does not deny the role of the "warrior side" or the value of fighting, but insists also upon the fact of weakness—there is debilitating, devastating, unproductive fear of the kind we hope to forestall in one another when we say "Don't be afraid" as a form of encouragement. But there is also a healthier, more realistic fear that can even, she suggests be helpful insofar as it refuses false comfort, bravado, and the particular fatigue of resistance, like trying to face down the oncoming wave rather than diving into it.

The plea with the "warrior side" not to be disappointed alludes obliquely to a common dilemma in relationships between the sick and their caregivers: the desire to show visible improvement in grateful response to their ministrations, to please them, to comfort them, can impose a curious social obligation upon the very sick. Adam Mars-Jones writes about this particular pressure in "Slim," a short story about a person with AIDS who tries hard not to disappoint the caregiver who comes to see him, always hopeful of some observable improvement:

> One of the things I'm supposed to be doing these days is creative visualization, you know, where you imagine your white corpuscles strapping on their armour to repel invaders. Buddy doesn't nag, but I can tell he's disappointed. I don't seem to be able to do it. (Mars-Jones, 6)

Such lingering desire to please is one of a variety of ways in which illness may carry with it a certain pressure to perform.

The final paradox in "Vulnerable" shows how fear can open the way for hard and important realism. If pain and death are indeed inevitable, taking full account of that inevitability can eliminate the waste of time and energy spent in specious consolations and conserve that energy for the business of equipping oneself to live through what cannot be avoided. They too the speaker implies, have their possibilities, which can't be explored if they aren't acknowledged.

Lynn Goldfarb's poem "Still" approaches fear in a context of confident defiance (Goldfarb, 207). Facing confinement to a wheelchair, the speaker insists on taking her own time to succumb to that necessity. Reading the title as the first line of the poem underscores her intention to claim every possible day of mobility before giving way.

Still

At home
I still walk.
Doctors, looking
down at me, say
YOUR SPINE IS DISINTEGRATING,
STAY IN THE WHEELCHAIR OR ELSE.
Or else what? I'll never walk again?
Never stand up? Of that,
I am not afraid.
I am afraid
of sitting down
for the last time.

So,
I still walk at home.
Unlock the door,
wheel inside, then
up:

My remembered feet
on the cool slate,
my gaze straight
into Gran's painted eyes.
Someday, I will have to look up
to remember . . .
or take her down with me.

For now
I still walk at home.
Nothing fast, nothing fancy.
Nothing
but one foot in front of the other,
which is everything, really.
Everything, if you appreciate
the shift of weight from heel
to toe, the way your arches
sigh into the carpet, and
the small dance that happens
when you just stand still.

Still // At home / I still walk. She declares. She has not yet been either confined to a chair or hospitalized. As long as she is at home, she is in charge of her condition, at least to a degree: she can calibrate her own pain threshold, her pace ("Nothing fast, nothing fancy") the goals she sets herself—standing eye to eye with her grandmother's portrait, for instance. By the end, "still walk" has taken on a new meaning, walking reduced—or perhaps distilled—to the "small dance that happens / when you just stand still.

   The three stanzas trace a journey from the threshold where her she resumes the authority she has had to relinquish to admonishing doctors to the center of a room she can navigate and occupy in her own way, in her own time. In the first the speaker, presumably returning from a visit to those doctors, takes stock of her strength, her continuing losses, what she has left, what her options are.

She admits to her fear, but not the fear they, or we, might think. In the second she acts, recognizing as she does so how what was once reflexive, easy, and unconscious now requires memory, effort, and determination. The third begins provisionally, as Annie Stenzel's poem ends: "For now." Now is what she has. Now is what we all have—"everything, really," as she says—putting one foot in front of the other. As she articulates her situation it becomes a parable.

The remarkable twist on the theme of fear in this poem reminds one of Roosevelt's adage that "the only thing we have to fear is fear itself." Being "afraid to sit down for the last time, the speaker insists, is different from being afraid of never walking again, never standing up. It's a find distinction. "Never" is one thing; not this time is another. Each time she stands, she claims a whole, still moment of living as a person who can walk. Not only is she that, but she is a person who has learned to appreciate the subtlest joys of walking—the "shift of weight from heel / to toe," arches that "sigh" into the carpet, and the specific tensions of muscles that keep her upright and still.

The grim prognosis "never" doesn't scare her. It appears to be inevitable. But the day to accept it hasn't come yet, and what she is afraid of is the failure of nerve that might hasten the day, turning the prognosis into self-fulfilling prophecy. She is afraid of failing herself, and perhaps the grandmother she remembers, by going too gently.

Meeting "Gran's eyes" mid-poem, the speaker takes the measure of her determination to have all the mobility left to her, every day of it, by rising to the level of a woman whose image in ways we are left to imagine signifies a challenge to be risen to. The ominous phrase "take her down with me" could, of course, refer to moving the picture once her eye level has changed, but might also suggest that "Gran" is the companion she will need, and have, to see her through when she can no longer stand—that the memory of one strong woman strengthens another.

Dancers, actors, practitioners of yoga or Tai Chi or Qigong or any number of other disciplines of the body know the truth this poem tells—that deep, slow, minute attention to the way muscles tense and skin meets floor and toes spread and arches flatten and rise is a source of self-knowledge and a way of centering and can provide the mindful mover with deep moments of rediscovered pleasure in the gift of the body—even a body that, finally, disintegrates and is still.

The actuality of known pain elicits a very different kind of fear than that of an insidious illness like cancer that often announces its presence only belatedly, having evaded the body's early warning systems. The suspicion of cancer and the tests that determine its presence and extent span a waiting period that is almost always colored by fear. Sandra Steingraber's "Waiting for the Lab Reports, Thinking of Penelope," a poem written in the course of her own cancer treatment, invokes the mythic image of a woman patiently weaving and unweaving her tapestry, putting off the moment when a decision will be required of her, hoping for the return of her husband to reestablish the stability of her household (Steingraber, 15). The highly literary trope contextualizes the poem against the backdrop of an ancient story of a woman who knows her dependence on powerful men, but also finds subversive ways to serve her own purposes. Steingraber, trained by education as well as by illness, has become a celebrated advocate for recognizing environmental links to cancer and reproductive health. In addition to publishing and speaking widely on cancer and toxicity, she once passed around a jar of her own breast milk to delegates at a UN briefing on dioxin contamination of breast milk (Steingraber, online).

In the poem, Penelope is besieged by suitors and obliged every day to find ways to put off their importunate bids. Her life, land, and marriage are at stake. So she weaves and unweaves a tapestry, promising that when it is done she will choose a new husband. It is a story about a woman of wit, shrewd and resourceful under ongoing threat, that embodies beautifully the idea that wisdom can negotiate with, forestall, and even defeat fear.

Waiting for the Lab Reports, Thinking of Penelope

Outside it stops raining.
I weave and unweave the ribbons
of my nightgown. A nurse
presents breakfast and leaves.
My mother comes to braid
my neglected hair.

The activities therapist
brings yarn and a needlepoint canvas:
a stiff red cardinal in a tree branch.
Someone who has been crying all night
is still crying.
Outside it starts to rain.

I must have been fourteen when
I first learned how Odysseus' wife
bought time. Unweaving:
the widening part in a woman's hair.
Chemotherapy: and the whole dark
tapestry unravels, the bird's
black feet unthread the black branch
and fly away.

Penelope, did you see them
in the operating room—
their blue masks, gathering closer,
our suitors, their urgency?

Between the opening and closing lines of the first stanza that mark the end of rain and its beginning again, the speaker chronicles her stay in the hospital with a series of images of weaving into which are woven other allusions to activities that seem aimlessly repetitive. No one is going anywhere. What is happening goes on happening—the weaving and unweaving, the doubtless unappetizing meals, the crying. And the cardinal on the canvas will never fly. It seems a scene of stasis, paralysis, unresolved apprehension, a stay of execution.

The metaphor of "unweaving" becomes more explicit in the second stanza, where it serves as an image of a life undone by illness, a devastating treatment, and a sense of losing hold on life signified by the bird who departs, leaving its branch clawed and frayed. No longer a harmless, static image, as in the first stanza, the bird taking flight suggests life departing, leaving the body bereft and damaged.

The final stanza shifts from explicit literary allusion to a more intimate engagement with the figure who offers the speaker a grounding point and a way of imagining her situation. Like Penelope's suitors, who hover like jackals, consuming her resources, eager to hear that Odysseus is dead and the prized woman available for marriage, the surgical team seems to her a little too eager, too ready, too hurried to leave time for her to wait for all the returns to be in, all possibilities explored before an irreversible decision is required of her—before, as another poet put it, she must "give" herself to them.

The fact that the poem ends with a certain whimsy, as the speaker aligns her situation with Penelope's in life-giving solidarity, suggests a healthy sense of possibility. She has decisions to make. Institutional urgencies notwithstanding, even the pressure of surgeons' schedules and the cascade of events likely to follow pathology reports and diagnosis, she can retain authority over her own destiny, she realizes if she bides her time creatively. The image of a determined, self-directed woman who would not be bullied into forsaking her own timing and purposes empowers the speaker even as she acknowledges what looms ahead. Stories do empower, and characters who provide a vision of what right action may look like, when they serve as templates for patients' own development of personal strategies of survival.

Poet Eamon Grennan finds an imaginative resource in myth as well, but less allegorically, and in a darker vein. Disease touches him—melanoma begun in the "touch" of sunlight—and death looms in the ambient air, "as if a myth had fallen / into the back garden / and stood in my light / when I took out the trash" (Grennan, 41). The large frame he throws around his diagnosis, the sense of cosmic forces at work in his body, offers a certain comfort in linking his story, that has come to such a critical turning point, to a much larger tale of the death and survival of other creatures, called out of darkness into light that is sometimes harsh and harmful. His poem recognizes fear as one of multiple ambiguities that confound the newly diagnosed.

Diagnosis

To be touched like that
from so far, collusion
of skin and sunlight—one
ray, one cell, the collapse
of fenceworks: I feel mined,
nicked like a leaf
to a brown spot of burn
that catches the eye. Visited.

With one eye open
I probe the small swelling,
hoping to know
this intimate enemy
that bites through the bone
if left to its own
staggering devices: so this—
as if a myth had fallen
into the back garden
and stood in my light
when I took out the trash—
is it. Detached
and absolute, the word
comes over the phone
and day chills a little, ghosted,
goes briefly out of focus.
Somewhere a knife is sharpening;
my skin shivers. I can
see my own skin
as if it were
another—a dear
companion, lover, brother—
shivering, Malignant.

Outside
I'm swimming
through a hot storm
of light: head down
I hurry from shadow
to shadow, eyes on the ground,
where I see the fresh tar
sealing the driveway
is already cracked open with
little craters, irresistible shoots
of dandelion and crabgrass
knuckling up. Nothing can stop
their coming to a green point, this
hungry thrust towards light. Here

are seeds the songbirds will forage
as the weather hardens
before snow, green wounds
gleaming in tar, life itself
swallowing sunlight. The blacktop
glares at a clear blue sky
and in my eyes the sun
spins a dance of scalpels:
I pray for cloud, for
night's benign and cooling
graces, to be at ease again
in the friendly
land of shadows.

The poem opens with a brief, factual, scientific description of what happened—UV rays invading the skin, breaking down cell walls—then proceeds to the speaker's felt response, as though he is a part of the earth, a plant, enduring the natural and inevitable destructions as they come. The final word in this stanza changes the terms of his reflection—suddenly the invasion, the penetration beyond the body's barriers, seems personal—an affront, a selection, a matter of some unspecified god's intention.

The theme of the personal invasion continues in the term "intimate enemy": the desire to know what is happening when cancer starts extends beyond biological or clinical information to a kind of knowing that is much more personal. Personification of the disease process as "enemy" is, of course, a common trope, empowering to the extent that it suggests the possibility of engagement, confrontation, battle, victory. That it "bites" through the bone turns the enemy to a vicious animal, and "staggering" makes it dauntingly large and powerful, mythic, and even monstrous. "So this is it" seems a death sentence, but the fanciful interruption makes the speaker seem more bemused than horrified.

The word "Malignant" that ends the stanza seems to take on a life of its own, as the cancer has, "detached" from a caring doctor's human presence, from the speaker's own life story, even from a body, coming as it does over the phone. That single word reframes everything—the day, the future, the speaker's relationship to his own body. Though he mentions the "cold" and "shivering," it is the day that chills, and the skin, but not the "I" who speaks, but who seems somehow separated from the sensations he notes.

The sensation of swimming reflects what seems to be a sudden change in the weather, temperature, the body's register of sensation. Light becomes unbearable, perhaps because what has been brought to light is so threatening. So the speaker seeks the relief of shadows. His gaze is downward toward the ground where the cracks and craters and weeds "knuckling up" mirror the slow destruction of his own protective systems from within. What has manifested as a small brown spot is a harbinger of more eruptions from roots that may prove intractable. Once cancer cells move from the innocuous looking skin spot into the lymphatic system or blood, the cancer often becomes intractable.

Noticing seeds "gleaming" in tar, taking in and reflecting the harsh light that now seems so alien, the speaker sees them not as signs of new life, but as sterile reminders of what remains only to be eaten. The blacktop "glares" at the sky—covering the earth as his skin covers his body, neither a protection against the force of the sun that here "spins a dance of scalpels." The vision of knives and scalpels of course signifies the speaker's fear of further invasion—the surgery that may or may not succeed in eradicating the spreading disease.

Ironically, the prayer that ends the poem is not for healing, but for temporary relief, refuge, darkness, shelter from sunlight and its exposures, since sunlight is now hostile and life-threatening. The speaker envisions the life he has now as one to be lived, literally, in the shadows—only a step away from living among the shades.

Lucille Clifton's poem of the same title, "cancer," ends on a similar note: the speaker seeks refuge in the darkness of a movie theater where the harsh truth of what she has now to face may be at least temporarily evaded (Clifton, 26). Her poem focuses more directly, however, on the waves of visceral response to a diagnosis that, though by no means inevitably terminal any more, still sounds like a death knell when the word is first delivered.

> cancer
>
> the first time the dreaded word
> bangs against your eyes so that
> you think you must have heard it but
> what you know is that the room
> is twisting crimson on its hinge
> and all the other people there are dolls
> watching from their dollhouse chairs
>
> the second time you hear a swoosh as if
> your heart has fallen down a well
> and shivers in the water there
> trying not to drown
>
> the third time and you are so tired
> so tired and you nod your head

and smile and walk away from
the angel uniforms the blood
machines and you enter the nearest
movie house and stand in the last aisle
staring at the screen with your living eyes

This poem traces early stages in the "journey" from diagnosis to treatment that most cancer stories articulate in some way: disbelief and a sense of surrealistic dissociation from the ordinary world; fear, entrapment, isolation, and over-whelm; weariness, reluctant acceptance, strategies of escape. The stages and strategies vary, but the successive waves of reaction, each one breaking with its own force and undertow, are a common feature of those stories.

The curious synesthesia in the image of the word banging against the eyes rather than the ears, and the visual hallucination that follows provide a forcible sense of not only psychological or emotional, but also physical disorientation. The body responds to the news with its own neurological arsenal of defenses.

But fear gets by our fortifications. It is a shape-shifter. It masquerades as confusion, alienation, fatigue, or apathy. The defensive strategies it generates are legion. And even the most rational fear also has elements of irrationality, reactivity and illogic. A single word triggers it here, and the speaker's attention is compelled not toward the facts of her case, the statistics, the prognosis, the possibilities, but toward the feelings that themselves require strenuous manage-ment.

The second-person direct address makes the poem more explanatory than confessional, as though the speaker is imparting inside information for the ben-efit of those yet to step through this looking glass. It reminds the reader, albeit obliquely, that many of us will be wrenched out of the stream of ordinary life and find ourselves in that twisting room or tumbling down that well of loneli-ness. It is a warning, but also, in its way, a gesture of comfort: the speaker has survived to tell this unsettling tale, has organized it into stages and stanzas. The orderliness of the telling works strongly against the fearful asymmetries of unpredictable moments of dread, and makes them predictable—a kind of ser-vice to the next one to be blindsided by the one-word diagnosis that stops the presses and radically redirects all one's energies to the project of living through rather than living on.

It seems appropriate to end a chapter on fear with a widely read poem—really a paragraph, but often reproduced and read as a poem—by a cancer survivor that begins with the strong, clear joy of the phrase, "I am no longer afraid..." Deena Metzger's words, often published with a photograph of her naked upper body, one-breasted and decorated with intricate vines tattooed over the mastectomy scar, invoke another mythic image as a source of strength and newly achieved identity—the amazon—the ancient woman warrior who cut off one breast to enhance the precision of her archery (Metzger, online). This gift to the breast cancer community has been posted on resource sites like oncolink.org, personal blogs, political blogs advocating health care reform, sites of feminist groups, and the online *Cultural Weekly* where it was posted to commemorate the death, and the courage it took First Lady Betty Ford to speak publicly about her own breast cancer as well as her addictions.

> I am no longer afraid of mirrors where I see the sign of the amazon, the one who shoots arrows.
> There was a fine red line across my chest where a knife entered, but now a branch winds about the scar and travels from arm to heart.
> Green leaves cover the branch, grapes hang there and a bird appears.
> What grows in me now is vital and does not cause me harm.
> I think the bird is singing.
> I have relinquished some of the scars.
> I have designed my chest with the care given to an illuminated manuscript.
> I am no longer ashamed to make love. Love is a battle I can win.
> I have the body of a warrior who does not kill or wound.
> On the book of my body, I have permanently inscribed a tree.

The lines offer a stirring and convincing record of transformation. The simple opening phrase, "I am no longer afraid" is a powerful testimony to the speaker's active reclamation of a life it once took courage to take up again. The scarred chest after mastectomy becomes a canvas on which to inscribe her insistent intention to take the life that is hers still, and give it beauty. The tattoo, visible on a widely published poster known as the Breast Cancer Warrior poster recalls similar acts of creative resistance to diminishment: Michelangelo designing the David around a flaw in the marble; Hester Prynne embroidering the scarlet A intended as a humiliation with gold thread in "fantastic flourishes"; men and women attaching balloons to decorated wheelchairs in a city's annual "disability pride parade." The one-breasted amazons have given her what she needs: a vision of a way to transform disfigurement with loving kindness, intention, creativity, and imagination. And so the scar becomes a branch—an archetypal image suggesting a deep life source. It extends "from arm to heart," linking power and love. Gradually, successively, leaves, then fruit, then a bird "appear" on the branch, the verb suggesting that, once begun, the process of elaborating the life-giving image takes on a momentum of its own. That she "thinks" the bird is singing is an indication that something she has begun has taken on a life of its own, or participates in a life she does not control.

With clarity and certainty the speaker proclaims a series of affirmations that establish the truth of her life now as warrior rather than victim. Where disease has been is a spot now marked and covered with signifiers of a force more powerful than cancer. She is no longer weak, she is no longer ashamed, as she is no longer afraid. She has inscribed a text of life on the scroll of her body as a sacred story. The poem ends on a note of triumph by sounded by a peaceful warrior whose battles are spiritual, though very much of the flesh.

On her website, Metzger, who is also an essayist, teacher, and leader of healing groups, posted these thoughts in response to a question she raised with a group of women: what does it mean to be a healer in the twenty-first century?

> Recognizing that illness is a complex story and that story provides meaning and that meaning and healing are interconnected, vitalized our lives. . . .
>
> We were also reeling with the new incidences of cancer and auto-immune diseases, as well as rape, abuse and other social diseases that were requiring us to understand illness differently. We began to re-

examine our understanding of the causes of various illnesses, and so also we re-examined our responses – emotionally, politically, environmentally and spiritually. . . . We began to ponder the connection between fragging, friendly fire and auto-immune diseases. We saw that there might be mysterious connections between inflammation and an enflamed world. (Metzger, online)

The larger picture, these days, is bleak. Yet it still provides perspectives on one's own illness that can be not only healing, but inspiring, giving a sense of purpose, meaning, connection, and mission to those who, having emerged from a cauldron of mortal fear, are not afraid any more.

Chapter Six
A Solitary Journey

I'll come again Tuesday. Our Dad
Sends his love. They diminish, are gone.
— U.A. Fanthorpe, "After Visiting Hours"

Isolation can be worse than pain. Not only in uninspiring hospital quarters or rumpled beds in untended rooms, but in the inexplicability of pain that can't be made into a narrative that feels worth telling, in the tedium of discomfort or dread or depression no one seems to want to hear about any more, in the alienation that led Flannery O'Connor to remark that sickness is a place you go and no one can follow you there (O'Connor, 163). No matter how big the community of kindly people attending the sick or disabled person, at some level illness, pain, disability, and dying are solitary journeys to be traveled with burdens no one else can carry.

D. H. Lawrence's 1916 poem, "Malade" speaks from the sickbed, offering a point of view of one temporarily shut away from the day outside in a "grey cave" (Lawrence, 112). The only form of suffering named in the poem is "confinedness." Whatever the illness, very likely influenza, which the poet suffered more than once, it is the sense of being cut off from the flow of life that most acutely weighs on the speaker in this memorably bleak and vivid poem.

Malade

The sick grapes on the chair by the bed lie prone; at the window
The tassel of the blind swings gently, tapping the pane,
As a little wind comes in.
The room is the hollow rind of a fruit, a gourd
Scooped out and dry, where a spider,
Folded in its legs as in a bed,

Lies on the dust, watching where is nothing to see but twilight and walls.

And if the day outside were mine! What is the day
But a grey cave, with great grey spider-cloths hanging
Low from the roof, and the wet dust falling softly from them
Over the wet dark rocks, the houses, and over
The spiders with white faces, that scuttle on the floor of the cave!
I am choking with creeping, grey confinedness.

But somewhere birds, beside a lake of light, spread wings
Larger than the largest fans, and rise in a stream upwards
And upwards on the sunlight that rains invisible,
So that the birds are like one wafted feather,
Small and ecstatic suspended over a vast spread country.

The three stanzas of diminishing length trace a succession of observations that begin with close-ups of objects in the room where the speaker lies restless and disengaged. The poem begins with an almost comic projection of sickness into the grapes that "lie prone" and uneaten, drying and unappetizing, depleted and no longer able to nourish. The only movement in the room is the tapping of the tassel on the window pane in response to a breeze—a measure of the ambient stillness, the dead air, as stifling as the pungent slow fermentation of an empty rind—an image suggesting pointedly that the "juice" has gone out of the place, the day, the mind that seeks occupation but cannot sustain focus, the body whose energy has been sapped.

As the speaker's gaze falls on the spider, he projects onto it, as onto the grapes, something of his own condition: it sits "folded in its legs as on a bed" watching with him the "twilight and walls" that seem to have obliterated all other stimuli. He is like the grapes, the spider, the pointlessly tapping tassel hanging useless, the hollow fruit, each image suggesting a different kind of lassitude, aimlessness, or decay.

The second stanza shifts from restless apathy to impatience. The sarcasm of the opening line works like a hand flinging back the covers or waving away all appeals. The whole atmosphere is a blanket of grey that falls like dust on each living and nonliving thing. The greyness gives a palpable sense of how one's own psycho-physical state can permeate ambient space and almost literally drain the color from the visual field. The sensation of "choking" the speaker names intensifies the impinging, suffocating oppressiveness, as though what has been projected outward is now breathed in, filling and thickening lungs and throat. The body seems to be absorbing what it emanates.

From this solitary sick chamber escape finally offers itself in memory and imagination. As the speaker envisions birds rising from a lake in a rain of sunlight, the poem itself opens and rises into a beauty surpassing in its pervasiveness and intensity the permeating greyness and decay that unfolded in the first two stanzas. To remember this scene is to reattach to the beauty and life it represents. The stanza reasserts the healing power of the imagination that can afford refuge and respite, at least for a time, even in the midst of sickness.

A similar and more recent treatment of the isolation of illness, Nancy Mairs' 1978 poem "Diminishment," written six years after she was diagnosed with multiple sclerosis, focuses on the sense of disengagement that grows as the body becomes less and less able to carry out the functions that give it a place in the active world, where, as Mandy Dowd put it in a poem cited earlier, "the busy lives swirl." The speaker locates herself as an observer who watches her own body recede, her vantage point still that of someone who has a life apart from the diminishing body, connected to the world of the living and very much aware (Mairs,16). The awareness lends her observations potent dramatic irony.

Diminishment

My body
is going away.

It fades
to the transparency
of amber
against the sun.

It shrinks.
It grows quiet.

Small, quiet,
it is a cold
and heavy
smoothed stone.

Who will have it
when it lies
pale and polished
as a clean bone?

Having lived with, and written about her experience of, multiple sclerosis for years, Mairs knows well the range of nuance necessary to situate oneself socially as a person with a visible disability. Her early essay, "On Being a Cripple" introduces a courageous note of comedy into an otherwise sober reflection on adaptations and language:

> I don't care what you call me, so long as it isn't "differently abled," which strikes me as pure verbal garbage designed, by its ability to describe anyone, to describe no one. I subscribe to George Orwell's thesis that "the slovenliness of our language makes it easier for us to have foolish thoughts." And I refuse to participate in the degeneration of the language to the extent that I deny that I have lost anything in the course of this calamitous disease; I refuse to pretend that the only differences between you and me are the various ordinary ones that distinguish any one person from another. But call me "disabled" or "handicapped" if you like. I have long since grown accustomed to them; and if they are vague, at least they hint at the truth. Moreover, I use them myself. Society is no readier to accept crippledness than to accept death, war, sex, sweat, or wrinkles. (Mairs, "On Being," 20)

Interestingly, in the essay, published eight years after the poem, she writes in a more seasoned reflection about the difference between her attitude toward her condition and that of the medical professionals who treat her, "I may be frustrated, maddened, depressed by the incurability of my disease, but I am not diminished by it, and they are" (Mairs, "On Being," 20).

Their "diminishment," which she understands as a sense of failure or even fatalism at the inability to cure the disease she brings them, distances them from her in her vigorous efforts to adapt physically, psychologically, and spiritually to what she knows perfectly well is to be a lifelong condition with an uncertain developmental trajectory.

In this earlier poem, however, her mode of address is far more spare, stark, and apprehensive. The poem consists of an observation, an extended metaphor, and a poignant question. The opening lines tell a simple, literal truth about physical atrophy after years in a wheelchair, and also, unavoidably, speak of death as an endpoint to the "diminishment" that seems it can't go on indefinitely. "Fades" specifies the body's "going away" as a gradual process, a function of forces as natural as the sun. Entrapment in "amber" evokes the jarring and apt image of an insect, dead and preserved—an object of entymological interest, and even of beauty, perhaps, but unliving. The following two simple sentences, each on its own line, try out other verbs, as though the speaker is in the process of tentatively identifying what is happening to her as it happens, and hasn't yet arrived at a definitive way of putting it. The tentativeness reminds the reader of the subtlety and complexity of the experience, each verb not only adding a dimension, but a new way of framing the process.

Imagined as a "smoothed stone," the body is a possibly lovely, but weathered fossil, what remains after natural forces have worn it smooth, lacking the edges and characterizing detail it might once have had. "Cold" and "heavy," lead us further toward reflection on the body as a remainder, and on death as a gradual process that begins in the midst of life.

The final question is childlike and articulates a core fear, not of death as such, but of loneliness: Who will want me? Who will have me? At what point will I no longer be lovable, desirable, worthy of being claimed?

The final image of a bone when the body has "faded" away entirely suggests archaeological remnants, relics, the residue of a life that has reached the endpoint of long diminishment. It is a complex image not only of death, but of utter aloneness: the bone is pale and polished and clean—a thing of its own austere beauty, perhaps of archaeological interest—not, in other words, nothing. It is a relic of a life lived, perhaps even a sacred relic. As the end point of the poem, it invites reflection on the descent into loneliness of the person with a degenerative disease who, as her abilities dwindle and her needs grow greater, becomes an "object" of others' attention in ways that can overshadow others awareness of her as subject. She may be an object of respect as well as pity, of both clinical and social interest, but increasingly, the speaker fears, one whose living is less conspicuous than her dying.

A complementary poem about the loneliness of the long-distance survivor, Diana Neutze's "Against the Odds" offers a glimpse of multiple sclerosis as a cauldron of spiritual struggle. Though she writes of herself, "I enjoy my own company and any autonomy I can still achieve," chosen solitude is very different from the isolation that comes with pain others cannot measure or comprehend. An essentially positive, life-affirming woman whose long spiritual practice of yoga has equipped her for a hard life assignment, she also writes, "The years of yoga and meditation have taught me to stand aside from what my body and mind are doing. This has given me a more charged awareness of what is happening around me so, although I am house/and wheel chair/bound, I am able to derive great joy in the little things of life" (Neutze, online).

Still, her creative writing is shadowed by an equally strong sense of the chiaroscuro of suffering—a truth without which the affirmations of enjoyment and acceptance would ring false. An Australian poet who, like Mairs, has lived with MS for many years, Neutze writes with similar frankness about how chronic, degenerative illness, involves one not only in physical adaptations, but in recurrent solitary Job-like confrontations with God to be worked out, if not in fear and trembling, certainly in frustration and uncertainty.

Against the Odds

It's all very well on a clear day
with silver birch leaves shining
and a hedge sparrow's song,
then God is easy.
It's very different on a pallid day
with high cloud
no contrast, no definition.
But how about the dark hollow
before dawn
when I wake in the straitjacket of disability
listening to the silence?

In the context of a series of poems about MS entitled "Downward Mobility," the title assumes specific metaphorical possibility: those who are ill "play the odds," in a sense. They are given "odds" of recovery, remission, long periods of stability, length of life, death. Here, though, as we learn at the end of the first stanza, the phrase refers to spiritual doubt. Illness isolates socially, but also theologically; many who fall ill or become disabled find their faith shaken, their faith communities insufficiently informed or interested, their inclination to pray or reach out to the God they thought they knew severely diminished. Some of the most acute isolation in prolonged illness is the inability to pray or to make contact with the "Higher Power" that fuels one's sense of adequacy, and even physical energy.

The "odds" of a God who witnesses human suffering—one's own suffering—and who cares seem high when all nature seems to "declare the Glory of God" and to "show forth his handiwork." But insofar as the practice of divine presence depends on the life, health, and beauty that testify to the "rightness" of creation, it can be impaired when those manifestations of beauty, goodness, and hope visibility and definition are hidden and befogged by pain, disfigurement, and paralysis.

Then the ante goes up on the question the poem leaves on the table: what do the odds seem to be in the lonely hours of early morning when the enormity of loss threatens to overwhelm and one wakes yet again to the imprisonment from which this life offers no escape? The question echoes that of Job's "comforters": "Where is your God now?" The final word, "silence" resonates with a history of human confrontations with divine absence from Job's railings to Jesus' cry of abandonment on the cross to Hamlet's final words, "The rest is silence." For a poet, though silence serves the same key function in poetry that rests do in music, words are sign and sacrament, capable not only of recording, but of imparting life. To listen into silence can be deep repose, restorative and generative, or it can be a horrifying dead-end of hellish isolation. Waking before sunrise, at the hour at which statistics say most of the dying die, to resume "the straitjacket of disability" it would seem, at least momentarily, the latter. Like Annie Stenzel, whose "An Incantation in the Small Hours of the Night" refers to the inchoate "thing" that "stalks" in the night, or Mary Bradish O'Connor, who reports similar nighttime terrors in the midst of living with cancer, this poet makes it clear that those small hours are full of darkness and absence—a quality of loneliness that not all the daytime visits of friends and caregivers can dispel.

Nor can others confer the gift of self-acceptance, no matter how much kindly, authentic social acceptance they offer. Part of the solitary struggle that comes with disfiguring disease is the effort to find new terms on which one may learn to love and accept oneself as one is. Not to measure oneself against unscarred, able, attractive bodies, or to shun one's own wounded body, not to internalize the feared, perhaps projected, judgments of others, and to come to terms with physical change and loss of normal functions takes both courage and time. The opening word of Nancy Louise Peterson's poem "I Entered the Room, Naked" situates a solitary, hard-won moment of daring as a turning point in her healing (Peterson, 3).

I entered the room, naked

finally brought the full-length mirror
to see my back,
shoulder blade to heel,
to see my front,
ankle to stitched chest,
trying to remember how they looked, those nipples,
up to my hair that will be gone, too, in a few weeks.
And I paid closer attention to the crease
in the back of my leg I hadn't noticed before,
the angle of the curve in my back,
the mole at the top of my thigh,
the wisp of hair around my lips.

I raised the jar to the flat of my head
and walked across the hardwood floor,
full of grace.
I caught a glimpse of the swan, her neck movement,
a glimpse of the lioness, her shoulder muscle,
a glimpse of this ancient one, her padded feet,
and I loved her.

Opening the poem with "finally" alludes to a whole back-story of dread and avoidance: the speaker is only now, after some time, willing and able to take stock of the actuality of her losses, the disfigurement of mastectomy, the gradual balding of chemotherapy. Alone, she takes a long, sober, intentional look, and gradually learns again to love the woman she sees—scarred, but beautiful and strong enough to endure the loss of breast and hair, those outward signs of femininity giving way to a new and deeper sense of womanliness identified with the animal grace and fierce beauty of the swan and the lion.

Her gaze goes first to the parts of her that are still intact—shoulder, back, ankle, then up to the "stitched chest" and the hair "that will be gone in a few weeks," taking in those physical features even as she recognizes a whole woman who is still whole and interesting in all the particulars of a body with its own still-distinctive features and story.

Learning literally to see oneself differently is a defining moment in healing. The challenge is to achieve a new construction of self that no longer depends upon the old measures of acceptability, normality, beauty, or wholeness. The verbs in the poem give us a sense of what that effort entailed. The speaker has "brought" the full-length mirror to a site she has chosen for this ritual encounter with self, perhaps out of storage, perhaps from another room to a private place where she can take the time she needs, unwitnessed, to perform this ceremony. The repetition of "to see . . . to see" insistently reiterates the sharp focus of her intention: this is what she must do to be saved, as it were; this is the next step in her healing. She must be willing to see, and no one can give her eyes to see herself with love and compassion; she must find her way to that grail of acceptance by taking a lonely journey from the darkness of denial into the light of full acknowledgement.

The next verb, "trying to remember," includes commemoration in the ritual work she is doing. No pretense is allowed. Remembering what is lost is necessary to recovery, not of what is lost, but of what the loss, for a time, shut down. Remembering how her nipples looked on the breast that is no longer there matters to her as it matters to someone whose beloved has died to remember a look on his face or a gesture. Conversely, she also "paid closer attention" to what is still there, "noticing" a crease on her leg, noticing the curve of her back, the mole, the wisp of hair like a slow litany of appreciation that offsets lament.

The next two verbs, "raised" and "walked," carry the biblical resonance of "Rise, take up your bed and walk," words spoken to a paralytic being healed. Raising the jar to her head, she also invokes the powerful image of tribal women carrying baskets and water pots on their heads, walking with dignity, balance, beauty, and strength on bare feet through hard places. Though she has not been crippled, she has been paralyzed in denial from which she emerges as she takes her first steps into a new state of "grace." In that state she "caught a glimpse" of a beauty and life energy she names in a pair of powerful animal images—the swan and the lioness—that open her imagination and heart toward the woman she now is, ancient and new, and she ends on the final verb that signifies the completion of this ritual journey and its reward: "and I loved her."

Naming in the third person a self she can now see in a new way retains a poignant, still careful distance between the self who sees and the self who is seen. There is in the final line a sense of wonder at discovery similar to that of a child discovering herself in the mirror for the first time with pleasure still tinged with confusion. To own and internalize that self when the mirror is gone is the next step of the journey. But a birth has taken place: the poem's title, "I Entered the Room Naked," carries its own biblical echoes of Job's "Naked came I from my mother's womb, and naked shall I return. The Lord gives and the Lord hath taken away…" Both those ancient words and this very current poem attest to the importance of the unencumbered, solitary, illusionless encounter with the self Lear identified when he complained that, "unaccommodated man is no more than such a poor bare, / forked animal . . ." (*Lear*, III, iv, 1), words that forthrightly acknowledge our utterly contingent condition, but also that in each of us that is unshakeable as long as we have life and breath, and retrievable even after life-altering illness and loss.

Peterson's poem is included in a collection called *The Cancer Poetry Project*, whose thematic table of contents maps a wide range of stages and attitudes common to people living with cancer. The first of these is "accepting a new body." The list includes other themes recognizable in many of the poems treated here—accepting death, anger, celebration, compassion, coping, denial, fear, grief, hope, humor, and—interestingly coming last—questioning. Like so many others, hers reminds readers that this sometimes muddy mix of feelings is not neatly divisible into "stages," but simultaneous, overlapping, confusing, sometimes exhilarating, certainly challenging. Moments of clarity like the one she arrives at in the line "And I loved her" are to be cherished and, ultimately, shared. But they often come in the enforced solitude of the small hours of the night or the room with a mirror, free of social expectation, free even of others encouragements when an "unaccommodated" man or woman can cry on the heath and then, expectantly, listen into a silence that is no longer dead.

Chapter Seven
In it Together

The world is too much with us, late and soon . . .
—William Wordsworth

Loneliness and isolation, as we have seen, are real and common aspects of pain and suffering. Sometimes overcrowding is, as well—too many people in and out of the room, too many phone calls, a surprising plethora of odd social obligations that come with illness or disability. Solitude is an unaffordable luxury for those who need constant care. One of the emotional paradoxes of suffering is that it brings both a need for others and a desire to be free of that need. Affliction can draw caregivers and patients into deep moments of intimacy, sometimes beginning long, companionable relationships. It can also breed irritations that are not easy to name or resolve, since they arise as a function of unavoidable encroachments, embarrassments, or inequities that separate the giver of care from the patient. Others' gazes, no matter how compassionate, may sometimes feel invasive.

Harold Bond's poem, "The Game," included in an anthology of writing by and about the disabled, "Despite This Flesh," focuses attention on things caregivers often miss and the frustrations those oversights can generate (Bond, 55). One reviewer paraphrases the core idea of Bond's poem in these words: "Killed by kindness, stifled by overprotection, choked by subtle if sometimes unconscious snubs, the physically handicapped are one of the world's most invisible minorities" (Miller, online).

These are strong verbs. The poem gets at strong feelings about others' responses to the speaker's suffering. Its complex tone is worth noticing for the way it navigates a murky area between gratitude and irritation, recognition of friends' help and resentment of their insensitivities.

The Game

You are my friends. You do things
for me. My affliction is
your hangup. It is yours more
than it ever could be mine.
You spread my affliction thin

enough to go around once
for all of us. You put my
coat on for me when I ask
you. You put my coat on for
me when I do not ask you.

You embrace my shoes with your
compassion. You tell me I
would be less apt to fall with
rubber soles. You carry things
for me. You tell me they are
heavy things, how it would be

difficult for anyone
to carry them. You open
mustard bottles for me. You
tell me how hard it is to

open mustard bottles. I
agree with you. I will not
destroy our game. At night I
dream I am Samson. I will
topple coliseums. I

will overwhelm you with my
brute power. I will knock you
dead. I will open mustard
bottles for you. I will show
you how easy it really is.

The poem introduces ambiguity immediately with the line-break after "you do things." No modifier identifies those "things" as good, helpful, or supportive. That friends "do things" leaves open the question so many ask of those who are suffering: "What can I do?" The hardest thing, sometimes, in the face of another's pain, is to do nothing—simply to be present. To avoid that, it is often easier to do "things." The third sentence darkens the tone further, especially with the word "hangup." The speaker recognizes himself as an object of others' anxiety, perhaps guilt, perhaps need to feel useful. He dares to name the uncomfortable fact that those in a position to help often take the occasion of others' afflictions to work out their own fears, needs, or ambitions.

The difference between help that is asked for and help that is not is key. That "help" involves delicate diplomacy is a matter the disabled often find themselves having somehow to teach those who want to help. That help is not always wanted, that help sometimes gets in the way, that it sometimes feels presumptuous or humiliating, that it can seem officious—all these matters are hard to bring to light, since the risk of giving offense is arguably greater for those whose needs impose new and complicated requirements on friends and family.

But there is room for a bit of laughter: the slightly comic note in "embrace my shoes" lightens the series of wry observations about the fussy maternalistic or paternalistic caregiving that is more condescending than the caregivers may imagine. The packages they carry, the mustard bottles they open, and especially the efforts to disguise those favors by suggesting the one who needs them is really no different from anyone else is the "game" that frames the speaker's observations. Among the games people play—a term for social transactions popularized by Eric Berne in his 1964 book of that name—are those that are designed to provide some unacknowledged gratification for the initiator, often under the guise of kindness or favor. A game, Berne writes, "is an ongoing series of complementary ulterior transactions progressing to a well-defined, predictable outcome.... it is a recurring set of transactions... with a concealed motivation... or gimmick" (Berne, 48).

The games he writes about, like the game Bond describes, may serve immediate purposes and avoid conflict, but are ultimately counterproductive.

So the poem ends on a note of frustration. The speaker dreams of proving himself, defeating the well intentioned others who see him so frequently in terms of his powerlessness. The verbs that describe his fantasies—"I will overwhelm you . . . knock you... show you" cast the transactions between caregiver and patient as a contest rather than an exchange. Still, the governing idea—that patients and caregivers find themselves involved in a social "game"—suggests also mutual participation, rules that enable as well as frustrate, and some satisfaction that is at stake for both parties. The poem cannot simply be read as a plea to recognize the game-playing and quit it, but rather, recognizing the game for what it is, to step outside it on occasion and clarify the terms of care—what help actually means to a given patient, what it may mean to honor the dignity of people who need perhaps to forgive the healthy and able-bodied for what one writer called their "bruising health."

Floyd Skloot takes a similarly critical view of misguided well-wishers in "Home Remedies," a long poem that takes on the tedium of prolonged illness and of the stream of advice it elicits. After developing Chronic Fatigue Syndrome in 1988, and with it a series of neurological dysfunctions, Skloot began to speak and write publicly about his condition, upon which he received a flood of unsolicited advice from friends and strangers, ranging from the commonsensical to the truly wacky (Skloot, 342). The poem is a series of dramatic monologues that represent the voices of advice-givers. It aligns the reader with the point of view of the hapless recipient of all these pseudo-medical directives. The serious purpose of this dryly comic poem is to invite us, as Bond's poem does, to recognize how others' efforts to help may add a complicating and burdensome dimension to what the sick must bear in order to get the attention and care they actually need.

Because the poem is longer than most included in this book, I have interspersed reflections on it between stanzas or sections. The full, uninterrupted text of the poem is printed in an appendix. Its cryptic epigraph introduces a provocative idea: even what seem purely biological or biomedical phenomena may have spiritual dimensions or effects.

> Virus: a Latin word meaning
> a poison that disturbs the soul.

This etymological citation introduces the poem as a reflection on the fact that sickness is never purely physical, and on the "disturbances" that come with illness. Then the poem opens with a tale of the harrowing sort often offered as a backhanded gesture of comfort to the sick: I know what it's like—believe me—I've suffered things you wouldn't believe!

> I
> When I was your age
> my liver got so sick
> I could feel it press
> the bottom of my heart.
>
> The virus that made it
> swell was large enough
> to see with the naked eye.
> When they drew my blood
> it was the color of urine.

"Really?" we can't help but think. This is the sort of self-glorifying medical horror story we recognize as a form of compensation for the tiresome and inglorious suffering one has had to endure. We consider the claims critically: since viruses can't be seen with conventional microscopes, let alone the naked eye, and blood the color of urine could only come from a cadaver, we have to decide here how much disbelief to suspend. Shall we humor the teller, settle back and chuckle over his exaggerations, or dismiss them out of hand? Or, perhaps, shall we attempt to listen to what lies behind the hyperbole? His extravagance identifies the speaker as one who not only wants to narrate an event, but to make an impression and offer help. The idea of illness impinging on heart space, for instance, works both literally and metaphorically, and introduces a strong invitation to reflect on the relationship between biology and emotion. The ensuing stanza opens its own questions about the power of the placebo effect:

> Then each morning I squeezed
> the juice of half a lime
> into a tall glass of hot
> water and drank it down.
> No virus can stand up
> to a lime. Two weeks
> later I was cured.

The obvious logical fallacies make this cure claim both appealing and humorous, and leave the reader considering, at least momentarily: maybe it was the lime! We are left to wonder with how many grains of salt to take in the teller's tale. The double-entendres work to various effects: The "squeezed" lime alludes back to the impingement on the heart, and makes "squeezing" an uncomfortably ambiguous idea. The idea of a virus "standing up" to the lime introduces a comic note that further complicates our sense of how to assess the speaker's story.

Extravagant, unlikely cure claims are a genre unto themselves. Instantaneous "natural" healings, faith healings, psychic healings, healings from odd and stringent nutritional regimens (like, for instance, hot water with lime) enjoy a spacious place in the geography of medical lore. Some seem inexplicably authentic. Many, like this one, appear patently ridiculous. But even the latter serve to raise a shadow of a doubt about the too-quick rationalism that says miracles don't happen, or that a food regimen can't obliterate a serious infection. This niggling doubt is reinforced when the tall tale turns into history:

> That was the summer
> of 1943 and I have
> not been sick one
> day since that time.
> My daughter has been
> on limes since she was
> weaned. It was better
> for her than any vaccine.

With the introduction of the date, "That began in the summer of 1943," the story becomes a history. What began as a remarkable incident has unfolded into an autobiographical narrative. First-person testimony, the record of experience, twice-repeated success is hard to dismiss, be the claims ever so far outside conventional wisdom. Odd things work. There's an appeal in the quirk factor. And a patient with a condition for which no real cure exists can easily find the fabric of critical rationality fraying against the tug of such appealingly simple remedies. Then comes the invitation:

> So my advice is try it.
> What have you got to lose?

The poem mimics the reasoning of people who invest faith in particular "natural" remedies without much context or complexity. And there's the rub, as Hamlet would say. What the cost of investing in unaccredited cures might be, however innocuous they may seem. "What have you got to lose?" is, after all, a question that carries a lot of freight. The lime cure may help; it may not; it may be a simple distraction; it may reduce our incentive to seek other treatment; it may diffuse our waning energies, leading us to invest hope and risk debilitating disappointment. The final advice in this first section works in two ways: you can't do much harm with a daily dose of lime, but also, you have, in fact, a great deal to lose if you invest too naively in single cures or claims of this kind.

Section II introduces another kind of extravagant claim. Moving from the virus to the electro-magnetic field traces a history of alternative medical claims that come from singular ideas, sometimes fears, and from a desire for simple diagnoses or solutions. The longing for explicability and a neat fit between problem and solution often results in this kind of reasoning. This section also introduces a new voice—another advice-giver, drawn, like Job's comforters, to the scene of suffering with a certain *Schadenfreude*, finding in it a ready occasion to play the expert:

> II
> I'm willing to bet your home
> is filled with electro-magnetic
> fields, which would explain all
> your symptoms: the fatigue, pain
> in your muscles and joints, brain
> problems. It is well known
> that static electricity causes
> a person's hair to straighten
> and makes you stumble on a breeze.
>
> I'm willing to bet you have
> a microwave, computer, Xerox
> machine and big screen tv.
> Your vision is getting worse
> because you sit right in front
> of the screen, not the other
> way around. Come to think
> of it, you probably use
> a curling iron on your hair.
>
> I'm willing to bet you live
> right under electric wires,
> maybe near a substation
> or radio tower. You depend

on the very things that are
killing you, my friend.
It's worth thinking about.

As the litany of pseudo-scientific possibilities grows, it becomes a little harder
to separate those worth serious investigation from those that are merely silly;
the jury is still out on the long-term effects of low-level radiation sources we
have accepted and normalized. Lest one miss the comedy, the associative con-
nection between the TV and the curling iron pushes the reasoning to an obvious
extreme that invites our laughter: it is another bet, another implied claim, an-
other general association from one "electrical" device with another. The relative
dangers of substations or radio towers are a little more threatening to many
people than TVs or curling irons.

Though the extravagance of this claim, like the previous one, makes it hard
to take seriously, the final warning has a prophetic ring and applies to a world
of invention extending well beyond medicine: the things we depend on are kill-
ing us. How enmeshed are we, we are led to wonder, in a web of devices and de-
sires that alter our consciousness, our consciences, our critical capacities, and,
indeed, our brains and our bodies? Like the question that ends the previous sec-
tion, this one continues to resonate. "It is well known" leaves the cure claim in
the indefinite space of passive attribution. The addressee, in this section, is the
one suffering from an undiagnosed condition. The claim about "static electric-
ity" appears to be logically connected with the claim about "electro-magnetic
fields." The speaker's willingness to "bet" makes explicit the role of speculation
in his assertions, but his definiteness about causality reasserts the authority of
his logic over against what might seem an obvious cause-effect relationship to
the addressee and the reader.

The third voice enters, fugue-like, with a prescription not unlike that of
the lime-pusher, but more elaborate, complicated, and invasive:

III
Peel a garlic clove by clove.
    Swallow them whole

one by one until you have
        to stop and then
dice the rest into tablets
        you can wash down
with raw milk. Rub them into
        creases of skin,
Grind them to powder and breathe
        them deeply in.
Wear long garlic amulets,
        take garlic baths,
burn garlic incense and drink
        dark garlic tea.
Morning and night you can try
        one dipped in oil
as a suppository.

The final claim, though, is serious, and its implications change the tone and raise a question: how much do we know about the devices we live with and what they're doing to us? The illustrations to this claim are rife at this point, so the comic suddenly turns both prophetic and portentious.

The rhythm of this section becomes chant-like. It is all in the imperative—a prescription, rather than a diagnosis—and the imperatives take on a ritual quality, inviting the one addressed to enter into a psychological state that bypasses rational analysis. "[U]ntil you have to stop" introduces a subjective dimension into the instructions: the patient will have to make a decision about his or her own tolerance levels.

The four ways of ingesting garlic: eating, drinking, rubbing on skin, and breathing, as well as wearing, bathing in, burning, and taking as a suppository become another comic kind of exaggeration—as though if one way doesn't work, another might. As though one can't get enough garlic. As though once the credulousness has begun, there is no end to the ways one might extend one's investment. The specificity of "long" amulets, or "morning and night" application, or "creases" of the skin come in comic tension with the apparent scatter shot approach of trying all ways to get garlic to do its healing work.

The comic effect of prohibitions increases as the poem goes along, spoofing the logic of elimination as an approach to healing. While many have been told to quit the earlier items in the list, the last ones—vitamins, fruit—begin to seem absurd. The logic of pollution extends finally to all outdoors, implying that nowhere is safe. The refrain works like a chorus, as the section becomes a cacophony of advice from them medical sidelines.

The tension mounts between successive reiterations of yet another extravagant claim, the recommendations escalating from reading and studying plausible testimony to taking responsibility for one's own healing to accepting radical redefinitions of one's biological and ontological condition, to trying what is evidently expensive, difficult, and dangerous on the basis of the extended logic that stretches further and further in the course of the poem.

Again, the single-substance remedy dilutes the question of the possible medicinal value of garlic by its outlandish extravagance. Billed as a magic bullet, garlic serves to caricature all nutritional claims. Garlic in every orifice, applied in time-consuming rituals, acquires unsavory associations with occult practices; the advice invites, indeed demands, a kind of total commitment at which even the most bewildered and desperate patients might balk. But the next stanza introduces a yet more daunting voice—the purist whose healing paradigm is a venerable regimen of elimination and purgation:

IV
Quit sugar
Quit vinegar.
Quit dairy.
Quit bread and flour products.
Quit corn
Quit caffeine.
Quit alcohol.
Quit chocolate.

Vitamins rev the body's motor so
Quit vitamins.

The worst thing is too much acid so
Quit fruit.

Anything that eats outdoors is polluted so
Quit meat,
Quit fish and fowl.

Taken singly, any one of these suggestions has a certain logical appeal—some more than others. There are good reasons to quit meat these days, but they have more to do with the conditions under which it is produced than the fact of eating outdoors. Oceans are polluted, and fish bear back to us the consequences of plastic dumps and oil spills. Too much of anything, including fruit, can create problems; sugar, dairy products, chocolate, caffeine, and alcohol can be found on the hit lists of many popular diets, even those carefully tested by nutritionists and medical researchers. But once again, the absoluteness of the speaker's claims turn medical advice into religious dogma, and forestall rather than inviting reasonable efforts to test the waters of nutritional advice.

The ante goes up again in the fifth section where the advice-giver, like a street-corner fanatic, simply hands out a tract with an apocalyptic warning: if you don't read this you may die. Your life depends on this particular information.

V
Please read the enclosed brochure
Please look over the enclosed testimonials
Please study this pamphlet

IT CAN SAVE YOUR LIFE

Heal yourself with nature's energy
Heal yourself with magnets
Heal yourself with nicotine

        IT CAN SAVE YOUR LIFE

You are the Lord's trumpet in His watchtower
You are not alone
You are allergic desensitized filled with empty of

        IT CAN SAVE YOUR LIFE

It's not expensive when you consider the alternative
It's not difficult if you really want to get well
It's not as dangerous as doing nothing

        IT CAN SAVE YOUR LIFE

Succinctly amalgamating the truth claims of all manner of fringe groups, along with their self-authorizing either-or assertions, their appalling certitude and their threat of blame for the reluctant, this section turns the chorus to a cacophony, eerily recreating the climate of bewilderment and fear in which the publicly sick may find themselves .

The next section takes on the popular methods of visualization, for which claims range, again, from the plausible to the absurd. Leaning rather more toward the latter, this speaker offers highly prescriptive guidance for healing meditations:

        VI
        Visualize little men
        in white coveralls
        Scrubbing the lesions
        from your brain.

Imagine a team
of climbers rappelling
the sheer face of your spleen
and see their axes chip
away the gleam of disease.

A phalanx of soldiers
trained in network
shows your weakened killer
cells how to kill again.

This is best done
in a darkened room
to the later music
of Dmitri Shostakovich.

Not only the images to be used, but the ambience to be created, have hardened
into dogma. Interestingly, this stanza foregrounds a feature it shares with all
those preceding: good, plausible sources of help turn counterproductive when
they are overgeneralized, oversimplified, and dogmatized. Therein lies a word
of warning as well for the purveyors of common prescription drugs: one size
does not fit all.

VII
To get well you must learn to heal yourself.
since every self harbors its own secret
cure, you must close yourself off from outside
influence and look deep within to find
what you need. My advice is to listen
to no one, not even your physician,
but rather go off to some deserted
corner of your own soul and lie beneath

its palms, letting the sun or your self show
you all there is to know about finding
the lost treasure of your own well-being.

The paradox of the solemn advice, "My advice is to listen / to no one" will not be lost on readers who have come thus far. Somewhere in the process the too-receptive patient may lose his own bearings and find himself floating rudderless in a sea of confusing and contradictory instructions, principles, logic, hopes. However true it may be, and this advice carries its own grain of truth, that one's healing may ultimately depend on a deepened self-awareness, avoiding advice is clearly a no more viable option than taking it indiscriminately. Sickness involves navigating the warren of paths traced by all the guides, inner and outer, with their competing and variable claims to credibility.

The final voice opens a new avenue of reflection, closer to home, perhaps, for the poet whose own illness has no cure:

VIII
Embrace your illness
like the day-old infant found
abandoned on a logging road
late one autumn morning
that was given its rescuer's name
when it was at last out of danger.

The final section takes on another widely recommended alternative method: visualization. The comic specificity of the last stanza is complicated by the fact that, if any of the methods suggested is plausible, they might well be done best to music. Shosatkovich's late music is complex, atonal, and difficult to listen to. Skloot, by his own testimony, used to do his writing to jazz, but after his brain injury couldn't work against any sound. So there's personal irony in the suggestion of doing this work to music. Music itself, in his own experience was once helpful, but now impedes the work he needs to do.

Thinking of the illness itself as something to be rescued from all the onslaughts, to be lived with and accommodated, to be understood and accepted as a source of learning may be the best option for the chronically ill. There is rest in this stanza; the contrast between this advice and all that has gone before suggests how a person might find respite and wisdom in "giving up"—at least in stopping the frantic search for cures that can turn illness to obsession.

The advice offered in this section is more ambiguous—not as evidently ironic as in the previous sections. It raises the question to what degree we might, in fact, be responsible for our own well being, to what extent self-knowledge, meditation, spiritual practice, might factor into successful healing.

A couple of the line breaks work to particular effect: the second line makes a claim of its own before it is changed by the word "cure" on the following line. We may be able to agree with the first assertion, but not the second. Still, the ambiguity raises the question what is the relationship between the first claim and the second.

"The sun or your self" is similar to the open-endedness of the term "higher power" used in 12-step programs. Whatever it is you seek or invoke in your own practice, the assumption is that there is an inner place of access to power that may be tapped. The final claim is not so extravagant as earlier ones: it may be that "well-being" is indeed retrieved or achieved in this way where physical healing may not be. The phrase "all there is to know" seems as extravagant as earlier claims on the face of it, but appears less so in light of the term "well be-ing," which is a condition that may not depend on physical healing or health.

The poem ends with a short stanza that develops a metaphor that overturns all the advice previously given. If all the advice doesn't work, what remains is to "embrace" and adopt what one was trying to eradicate. You can learn to live with the illness, accept it, adapt to it. This, too, is a kind of recovery. So "at last out of danger" may suggest that the danger did not inhere entirely in the illness. When it is no longer life-threatening, it may be that the incentive to seek a cure has a limit. And that "out of danger" may be that finally the voices cease and life may begin on new terms. Skloot answers the question about whether he will "get better" by simply stating that he will never be the man that he was; that he has learned to perceive the world more clearly and slowly since his ailment. In his memoir, *In the Shadow of Memory*, Skloot explains "I have changed. I have learned to live and live richly as I am now. Slowed down, softer, more heedful of all that I see and hear and feel, more removed from the hubbub, more internal."

The poem may be read as a series of stages in accommodation to illness. The bewilderment of advice given to the one addressed crests and finally comes to rest in the only advice he may be capable of acting upon. It may be read as a chronicle of hope, and how hope, rather than the object of hope, changes.

Though the exposures and tiresome intrusions may be a dimension of illness or disability that deserves more explicit recognition, the ways in which illness is always shared and social may also be recognized as an occasion to reinforce a simple and central fact about the terms on which we live and die: we're connected. Even in our isolation, we're connected in ways that are not always apparent, but are nevertheless important. We are accompanied both by those who care for us and by those who simply witness our suffering. Elizabeth Jennings' poem, "Diagnosis" describes a hospital encounter that evokes the speaker's empathy and deepens her own sense of connection to others who are suffering even as she is, but without any actual exchange with the woman to whose situation she is a silent and unacknowledged witness (Jennings, 34).

Diagnosis

The doctor talks. The students gather round.
I'm opposite this patient in a bed
close enough to hear each separate sound.
I heard each syllable the doctor said
but I am carefully bound

to seeming not to listen. Doctor goes,
students chat and smile and disappear.
That patient opposite is wrapped in fear,
she turns and pulls her sheets and blanket close.
I am so far though near.

The patient's name is Milly. Now and then
we've talked of trivial things. We've never said
a word about our illnesses. Her pain
is obvious to me. Will she be dead
soon? What does it mean

that operation which the doctor told
her wasn't 'very serious'? I knew
the very opposite was true.
I dared not show compassion and be bold
and tell her that I knew.

At length knowing I could not find the right words
to fit the time, I kept our talks upon
humdrum matters. She would point out cards
she had received. Her operation's soon.
O human nature's cards

ought to be tougher and more sensitive.
The very contradiction makes me see
how far we are from powerful sympathy.
I do not know how long that friend will live
but feel her lack in me.

The speaker's description of her own situation as one who overhears what should be a private conversation underscores a point made in the previous two poems: that illness and caregiving often involve unavoidable breaches of social protocol not easily acknowledged or rectified. In contrast to the doctor and medical students, all involved in their own professional agendas, the speaker aligns herself with the patient whose fear remained unaddressed by the medical staff who deliver their diagnosis, perhaps with an unsettling prognosis, and leave. She finds herself uncertain whether to presume upon the friendly but superficial connection she has established with her roommate, both of them temporarily and arbitrarily thrown into each other's lives, by breaking the silence between them, or to keep what she feels and "knows" to herself. No one has appointed her to be the truth teller, but important truths are not being told, and so she faces the question about who has the right or obligation to speak. She finally defers to decorum, but is left with an aching empathy and a sense of the tragic inhibitions that keep us from entering into each other's stories at such times to offer and accept the "kindness of strangers" that might make an incalculable difference in a patient's welfare.

Much caregiving, of course, involves authentic, long-term, intimate engagement of people who are already part of each other's lives, but who find themselves similarly baffled by the strangely inhibiting question of how to impart hope while also honoring the truth of loss. Murielle Minard's "Bedtime Story" recalls the ministrations of a mother to a child afflicted with polio, continued long after it was clear they were not "working," perhaps as a ritual of hope that echoed more hollowly over time (Minard, 56). Gently the poem leaves open the question what purposes may have been served by the nightly enactment of a healing ritual that did not heal, and with the question the first poem pointed to that all caregivers ask: "What can I do?"

Bedtime Story

Every night
my mother
would massage my legs
with melted cocoa butter
up and down.
Slowly—
faithful to the ritual,
she never spoke.
Only her strong hands
insisting.

We both
believed
it could undo
what had been done.

I do not remember
at what point
the ceremonies ended.

The title of the poem positions "story" as a frame for this account of a healing ritual faithfully carried out, but, practically speaking, futile. Like most bedtime stories, this one turned out to be a wishful fiction, perhaps serving authentic and important purposes—mother-daughter bonding, comfort, imparting love that equipped her later to cope with loss. But the cocoa butter didn't banish the effects of childhood polio.

That the mother "never spoke" is an important detail: the odds, the fear, even the hope, were very likely too hard or too frightening to communicate to a child; only her "strong hands" delivered those messages, along with a sense of collaboration in the business of getting better. Her silence was apparently part of the fidelity the speaker has come to understand: what the mother was doing was a sacred task, carried out like a priest's ministrations at the altar, without comment, with deep focus on the hope of transformation.

The second, short stanza is a simple statement of fact, still not naming the disease, but maintaining focus on the unifying hope shared in this little credo. The phrase "undo / what had been done" echoes the formula in a still widely used traditional prayer of confession: "we have done what we ought not to have done and left undone those things we ought to have done and there is no health in us." The simple words convey a longing similar to the longing for forgiveness expressed in that prayer—that a deadly progression of events might be reversed, unraveled, forgiven, and the momentum of sickness redirected toward health and wholeness.

That the final stanza begins with "I do not remember" emphasizes the contrast between the aching clarity of the memory she has written down and the release of a long-held childhood hope. At some point she relinquished it along with the other myths of childhood, having to give up hope of physical healing. Still, the poem foregrounds the memory of the loving ritual as the thing that remains. Only peripherally acknowledging disillusionment, disappointment, what remains is a memory of a healing act that remains a healing act, despite its apparent futility.

The ending is understated. The letdown into the concessions and compromises of adulthood was gradual, undramatic. Like loss of a childish faith (perhaps the sort of naïve hopes that Paul refers to in Corinthians when he mentions putting away "childish things" to make way for a more adult faith, hope, and love) the speaker recognizes that the "ceremonies" had to end. This poem, however, is a vestige of and tribute to that faith, and to the mother who saw her through in the only way she knew how. The polio left its ravages. But the comfort the poem commemorates came about by the insistence of "those strong hands." These may after all be among the best gifts caregivers can bring the sick, as all these poems suggest: uninvasive presence, silent companionship, willingness to witness and endure with them the uncertainties they face, a flexible hope that refuses the temptation to predict or advise, but takes on the hard daily business of being there.

Chapter Eight
Keeping On Keeping On

For us there is only the trying.
—T.S. Eliot

Among the poets who have left records of rage, acceptance, fear, cunning, wry humor or sobering reflection on life with prolonged illness, Lucille Clifton occupies a widely recognized place. Beginning with poems in *the terrible stories*, written shortly after her diagnosis with breast cancer at the age of 58, her legacy of poems about her disease and treatments empowered a widening audience of similarly afflicted readers over a period of sixteen years until her death in 2010.

After *the terrible stories* (1996) she made no effort to collect the cancer poems and publish them together, but let them emerge as part of a much larger corpus of poetry over those same years that include much material that is not at all about disease. The integration of the cancer poems with all the others reflects her determination not to make cancer or kidney failure defining conditions of a life richly lived, even in the midst of their ravages. Several obituaries reported her death "after a long battle with cancer," yet "battle" seems too simplistic a word for the steady courage, acceptance, bemusement, outrage, and exploratory curiosity evident in the lively voice she brings to suffering.

In Clifton's *New York Times* obituary, Margalit Fox wrote, "She could write unflinchingly of personal hardship, including being sexually abused by her father when she was a girl and her struggles with cancer and kidney failure as an adult. Yet, as critics remarked, she was steadfast in her refusal to cast herself as a victim" (Fox, NYT online).

And Gayle Sulik, in her reflections on cancer writing, remarks of Clifton's cancer poetry, "She emphasized the importance of memory in helping people to heal the wounds of life, not to rise above them but to travel with them" (Sulik, online).

"dialysis" traces the beginning of Clifton's adjustments in the immediate aftermath of treatment for cancer that involved both breasts and a kidney (Clifton, 16). Starting with a whimsical "report" of her condition, the poem situates us in a dialysis treatment room where shocking evidence of others' suffering is unavoidable. The speaker watches, registers, and takes the measure of her present experience by recalling what it was "supposed to" be like, finding it unsettlingly different from what she supposed: alienating, aggravating, the cure hardly more tolerable than the disease. It is a dream that turns her story from grievance and lament to bemused perplexity about the paradox she is left to live with, infuriated and grateful.

dialysis

after the cancer, the kidneys
refused to continue.
they closed their thousand eyes.

blood fountains from the blind man's
arm and decorates the tile today.
somebody mops it up.

the woman who is over ninety
cries for her mother, if our dead
were here they would save us.

we are not supposed to hate
the dialysis unit. we are not
supposed to hate the universe.

this is not supposed to happen to me.
after the cancer the body refused
to lose any more. even the poisons
were claimed and kept

until they threatened to destroy
the heart they loved. in my dream
a house is burning.

something crawls out of the fire
cleansed and purified.
in my dream i call it light.

after the cancer i was so grateful
to be alive. i am alive and furious.
blessed be even this?

The first line gives an abbreviated history of Clifton's own experience—first diagnosis and treatment for breast cancer, then kidney failure, a new loss, different from, not continuous with, the cancer. The strangeness of that loss becomes startlingly apparent in the curious image of the "thousand eyes," which casts the kidneys as beings with lives—and deaths—of their own. Alive, they "witness" the essential life processes of the body, bringing clarity and order to metabolic processes, situated at key check-points, protecting the coordinated systems—the "political life" of the body.

The second stanza jars us into the present moment: the speaker's own eyes, contrasting with the internal eyes that have closed, take in her visual field with chilling matter-of-factness. She sees the blood, the tiles, the mopping—now equally neutralized and neutralizing features of the institutional landscape she now inhabits. That someone's blood is the only "decorative" element she notices, and that it is quickly cleaned away, suggest how desperately the eye searches for something interesting, beautiful, lasting in this bleak place. Her moment of noticing is reminiscent of Toni Morrison's memorable character, Baby Suggs, who, when she is dying, longs for color. Against a barren winter landscape, all white and grey, she pleads, "Bring a little lavender in, if you got any. Pink, if you don't." And Sethe, who cares for her, "would oblige her with anything from fabric to her own tongue" (Morrison, 4).

After the eyes, the ears are assailed by the pathetic sound of suffering compounded by dementia. The cries of an old woman for her mother, futile and bewildered, remind the speaker of her own losses of those who, she wishfully thinks, might have saved her. But such a thought is as pointless and sterile as the cries of the old woman. They are not here, they would not be able to relieve the suffering if they were. Sanctified by memory, "our" dead could have done little more alive than they can now. It is a moment of magical thinking, a last, quickly disintegrating shred of the denial that softens rage into grief.

The three "supposed to" phrases that follow in succession signify a process of letting go—of expectations, of unexamined notions about recovery, of the sense of safety that health confers. The first two bespeak a felt solidarity with others in the dialysis room—the blind man and the old woman already introduced who are now her compatriots. The third is utterly personal. In her outrage and sorrow, the speaker reverts to an elemental, irrational sense of personal affront, losing momentarily the capacity for generous imagination that identification with others' suffering requires. It is a broad leap from the dialysis unit to the universe. The quick and radical change of frame suggests how total is the speaker's sense of change and loss. Nothing is, or ever will be, the way she once perhaps naively believed it would be, and planned for. The terms on which life was given have changed, and affliction extends not just to the body or even to the mind, but to the spirit that cries out like Job who curses the day he was born. Still, the line itself is not a curse, but a confession of naïve bewilderment. The "rules" of fair play that children tearfully insist on and that adults invoke in spite of themselves have been broken again. They don't, we are once more forced to admit, govern the universe or our social contract with God. If there is justice, it isn't the kind that guarantees good health to good people.

From these musings the speaker returns to her chronicle of what happened after the cancer, the cancer now being a defining landmark and turning point on her journey. Something in her was triggered into preservation mode, but ironically late. Like a hoarder afraid to let go of the things that encumber her life to the point of paralysis, the body clings to poison long after it has outlasted its questionably beneficent effects.

Ending with a dream, the speaker reaches beneath the surface turbulence of illness and tedious treatment to a dream space where all events have cryptic significance, and the conditions of waking life may be recast as parable. The burning house, the light emerging from the fire "cleansed and purified," suggest not just survival but transformation. The biblical and mythic archetype of trial by fire provides a frame of reference and a way of retrieving or assigning meaning that the speaker accepts. She arrives, and the poem arrives, at a concession to costly gratitude even in the midst of fury. The disease has redefined her life her world, her relationship with her body; even her unconscious has been recruited to cope with its destruction. It has also deepened the paradox: blessing and curse come from the same source. To live now is to live with loss, unable to take refuge in denial.

The final line echoes the power of Job's insistent "yet will I bless him" and the wrestling Jacob's demand for blessing as he limps away from his divine encounter weary and wounded, with a new name and a promise. Like those ancient forbears she has reached no conclusion, only a story that goes on unfolding, a life that will be harder now, and more uncertain, but in which it is still possible to speak, at least wryly of blessing.

Even in the long dry months of recovery and the dailiness of continuing disability moments of blessing may fall like small pieces of manna on a desert journey of indeterminate duration. Margaret Robison's "Five Months After My Stroke" offers a retrospective slightly more distant from the immediacies of diagnosis and treatment, but similarly cognizant of the surprises involved in the long, unsteady aftermath (Robison, 224). It begins in memory, but brings us to a present that is no longer charged with the shock of diagnosis or even of early recovery—milder, more open to possibility, more centered in the poets, and speaker's, achieved accommodations that have defied prognosis and allowed her a way to live richly in the open space of uncertainty.

Five Months After My Stroke

Five months after my stroke, and strawberry
apples fill the apple tree
growing by the river.
Five months after my stroke, and bees
hum in the oriental bamboo
that flowers on the riverbank.

"I cannot hold hope out to you," the neurologist said,
standing at the foot of my hospital bed
in which I'd lain for weeks, paralyzed,
unable to move my left arm, my leg.
"You should begin to think about a nursing home,"
my other doctor said. Sober. Grim.

All that day I struggled
with their words, with my body.
By midnight I sat clinging
to the bed bars. Upright.
Triumphant.

Now I've rolled my wheelchair to the open door.
And look—there's wind on the river today.
Wind in the trees. Wind
Shaking the leaves of the oriental bamboo
Shaking the sumac. The lilac. The beechen.
Knocking the ripe apples together.

The poem begins not with a reflection on the speaker's own health, feelings, or losses, but with attention to the natural world, framed now by a new sense of time as aftermath. The perspective provided in the opening stanza invites us to survey the nearby landscape as she does, noting signs of life, health, and renewal. The inventory opens with an image of hybridity: strawberry apples, an unusual variety of summer apples that grows in the Northeast, combine two tastes, and offer their own unusual sweetness. They ripen in September, just as the season is turning. That moment of ripening is here now: the tree is full and ready for harvest. The image of the tree growing by the river continues the note of hope in its evocation of an archetypal promise from Psalm 1 that those who are blessed shall be "like a tree planted by a river, bringing forth its fruit in due season." This tree is rooted in a place of abundance. It has all it needs for continuing life and health. The speaker takes in its health and promise like a particular gift this year—a living affirmation of what is rooted and grounded and good.

The stanza continues with reference to the time of year marked biologically both by the life of the speaker's damaged body and by the hum of bees in oriental bamboo, a sturdy plant with delicate stems, described by gardeners as "difficult to kill." It is one of the fastest-growing plants on earth, and may achieve full height in a single season. Most species flower infrequently, sometimes in multiple year cycles. All this suggests that the activity the speaker witnesses testifies to a very particular moment in both the seasonal cycle and the life cycle of beings obedient to the complex signals of a very particular environment. They offer very specific images of hope, but also of temporaneity: the moment is time-bound; this flowering may not happen again for some time. The speaker cannot climb to harvest the apples. She witnesses these life forms at their quiet work from an enforced distance that she cannot traverse as, presumably, she once did.

Still, the opening line of the following stanza is jarring in its blunt negation, courageous in its irony after the opening moments of quiet acceptance. The neurologist's words, "I cannot hold out hope to you," deliver a bleak forecast. Yet we have already seen that hope comes from other sources; it may not be his to offer or withhold. It may be that in the five months since his grim forecast and now, the speaker has transplanted her hopes in new soil. Moreover, his bad news, recalled from the distance already measured and marked in the first stanza, has been trumped by the apple tree, the bees, the flowering bamboo, and the one who has survived to tell about them.

The shift from present tense to simple past, and then to past perfect, in this stanza signifies a receding moment of loss and dread. The speaker has survived into a life on new terms, to be sure, but they are terms she continues to negotiate, and the doctor's dark prophecy continues to cast its shadow. She is not in the nursing home, but the thought of it, even rejected, leaves its after-image, not fully erased even by the beauties of home in September.

Weeks of paralysis came to a head in this encounter, which turned out to be not a moment of relinquishment, but a moment of decision, recounted in the next stanza, the place where poem and the life it speaks of take a decisive turn.

The decision to come home took time. The speaker's struggle with the doctors' words both fueled and compounded her struggle with her incapacitated body. The decision required an arduous challenge of their prognosis and their authority, and the force of will to reroute the brain's signals and recast its instructions to reawaken the dormant muscles. In that process what was once a thoughtless and commonplace act becomes a triumph: sitting, even though it requires fierce effort and the support of bed bars, is a first step in a new story of keeping on.

The final stanza brings us full circle to a present as triumphant as the upright moment in the hospital bed. The speaker not only sits upright now, but is mobile, able to reach a place from which she can witness and, to that extent, participate in life and beauty. Her loss, though not dwelt upon or even mentioned again, casts its *chiaroscuro* across the scene: the speaker may witness the conversation of life forms at the river's edge, but she may not go there. She is bound to her chair, and to a tyrannous constraint she cannot transgress at will. Her role is to watch from this distance what she might once have participated in by picking apples and trimming lilac branches or thinning the bamboo. Or just by walking qualified pleasure itself, generously shared in the invitation to "look" with her, reflects an act of will to accept the modified happiness given in her new condition, unlikely ever to return in full to what it once was. The ripe apples, unpicked, are knocked together by wind that will accomplish the harvest without her. Some will be bruised. Some will lie where they fall. Someone else will have to gather them. In the "Now," though, they are hers by courageous consent: what she is willing to enjoy, she can have.

The five months of survival from prognosis to this poignant September moment go unrecorded. What has transpired between the moment in the hospital bed facing the doctor's grim and sobering sentence and the moment in the doorway facing the cresting season from a wheelchair remain open to speculation. What matters, the poem insists, is now. The present moment is not simply a given, and perhaps never will be again, but an achievement to be celebrated, and a pleasure far more provisional than it once seemed, not to be missed.

A dimension of that achievement is resistance. The doctors did not have the final word. The hope they withdrew had to be retrieved by defying their authority in the solitude of a long night and steady persistence over five months, likely to be required in greater measure as time goes on. What it will require is implied in the word that describes what it took to sit upright in the hospital bed: clinging—to metal bars, to a revision of life in which deep pleasure is still available, to whatever supports are required to travel to the nearest doorway and look outward.

"Aftermath" may be a defining idea that stretches long into the life that remains after illness or loss. Richard Hugo strikes a very different note from Robison in a similarly retrospective poem that records a span not of five months, but of twenty-five years since the onset of treatment for crippling arthritis. The bold second-person direct address of "Hot Springs" brings the reader into an intimate psychological space that offers a privileged vantage point from which to take stock of a succession of false hopes, disappointments, losses, poverty, pain, and the inevitable aging that darkens and sharpens the ironies of ongoing treatment that eventuates in little more than uncertainty (Hugo, 75).

Hot Springs

> You arrived arthritic for the cure,
> therapeutic qualities of water
> and the therapeutic air. Twenty-five
> years later you limp out of bars
> hoping rumors will revive, some doctor

will discover something curative
in natural steam. You have a choice
of abandoned homes to sleep in.
Motels constructed on the come
went broke before the final board
was nailed. Operative still:
your tainted fantasy and the delux hotel.

You have ached taking your aches up the hill.
Another battery of tests. Terrible probe
of word and needle. Always the fatal word—
when we get old we crumble. They wave
from the ward and you creak back down
to streets with wide lots between homes.
When that rare tourist comes, you tell him
you're not forlorn. There are advantages here—
easy pace of day, slow circle of sun.

If some day a cure's announced, for instance
the hot springs work, you will walk young
again in Spokane, find startling women,
you wonder why you feel empty and frown
and why goodbyes are hard. You go out healthy
on the gray thin road and when you look back
no one is waving. They kept no record
of your suffering, wouldn't know you
if you returned, without your cane, your grin.

The opening line is crisply matter-of-fact, in the way of naïve hope that invests
in a promise and imagines a timely cure. "You arrived arthritic for the cure"
clothes the diagnosis in the simple syntax of fact. The second and third lines
are a similarly simple two-line inventory of therapeutic means: the water, the
air. Millions make this pilgrimage to spas and springs, investing in a legacy of

testimony, folklore, sacred story, and longing, and some, like this speaker, relive their own version of the cripple by the pool of Bethsaida who waits 28 years unhealed by the healing waters.

This speaker waits 25, carrying his disappointment and battered hopes to the places still accessible despite encroaching poverty and reduced mobility: bars, abandoned homes, an old motel. Among these, "You have a choice," he wryly points out. You still have a choice, so you take it.

By the time he arrives at these margins, hope has diminished to vague abstractions. What remains to be hoped for is that "rumors will revive," or that "some doctor / will discover something curative / in natural steam"—a far fetch, indeed, the distance of this wistful speculation from real hope measured in the repeated, tentative "some." Even as he speaks of his remaining hopes, he recognizes them as "tainted fantasy." Still, there is enough left of the real thing to move him up the hill for "another battery of tests" that entail the dual "probe" of word and needle. Like the speaker in the Robison's poem, this one identifies the doctor's words as instruments of pain. He speaks the fatal sentences: We age. We die. And some are not made whole.

Acceptance has become a way of life, but hardly as sanguine as that of the speaker who takes in the beauty of wind among the apples and lilacs. This one resides in a double-negative, that seems at best a half-truth told to tourists— "you're not forlorn"—and a short list of "advantages" to be enjoyed in this place where hope has been nearly abandoned. Even one of those, the "slow circle of sun," takes on an ominous sound, relentless prolongation rather of what is to be endured rather than expansion of time enjoyed.

The final stanza dispels false hope and denial in the strong light of realism. Suppose you were cured, and could walk the streets renewed and transformed by restored health. Those who knew you before "kept no record of your suffering," and would be likely to see only an aging man, whose able body is of no particular interest. Those who have known you in the long course of accommodation to chronic pain would not recognize you without the distinguishing marks that have become a signature—"your cane, your grin."

Streaked as it is with shades of grey, the poem may not be reduced to an act of resignation. Rather, it chronicles a long story of accommodation that gradually, and finally, comes to acceptable terms with what is. Like the triumph of sitting, clinging to bars of a bed, the poem constitutes an act of will that defeats despair. The speaker has consented to the "full look at the worst" that Hardy defined as the prerequisite to whatever "way to the better" might be found. In this full look, a radical revision of hope appears to be not much different from the concessions we all make to the aging body that "crumbles." And something almost jaunty in the cane and the grin suggest that strategies of accommodation themselves may yet open new ways to choose life and enjoy what is left.

In all these accounts of life in the aftermath, time seems to stretch or compress, widen or disappear like images in a carnival mirror. Barbara Ruth, a poet whose seizure disorder and multiple chemical sensitivities have kept her moving "back and forth from disabled to able-bodied since childhood," offers a profound reflection on how a disabled body changes the experience of time in "My Disabled Women's Group" (Ruth, 33). In that poem she recalls a particular moment when the difference between her time dimension and others' comes clear.

In My Disabled Women's Group

In my disabled women's group
the facilitator asked me
"What goals do you have
for yourself in the next five months?"
I felt the panic rise in me
thinking of the days
without a job
the weeks without the money
or the energy
to move my furniture
from the garage where it is stored
six hundred miles away
How many times will my stomach hurt
In the next five months?

How many times will I throw up?
How many times will I go to the welfare office?
In the last three weeks
I've been seven times, and still no check.
I remember articles I've read on time management.
How you plot out goals
for the next ten years
then one year
then six months
one month
this week.
Then you figure out
what you're going to do that day
and how it relates to the master plan.
I realize her question is quite reasonable
It's what other people do.
I don't live that way, anymore.
I divide the days into smaller sections—
A whole day is too much pain
too much responsibility to get through.
It started in the hospital
when I got morphine every three hours.
I'd watch the clock: the shot took 45 minutes to take effect
then I slept for an hour and a half
then 45 minutes till I could have another.
It's the way I passed the days.
Now, I divide it up with vitamins
I tell myself if I'm still awake at midnight
I'll take another C; calcium if I haven't got to sleep by 1:00.
I write down the things I have to do.
On a good day I'll have checked off almost half the list.
Five months from now? Maybe if I'm lucky
I'll be living then
a whole day at a time.

The interior monologue recorded here, triggered by the facilitator's question, becomes a long reflection, rich with detail, on how pain changes the way one lives in time. The speaker's first reaction is panic: five months seems an impossibly long stretch of time to contemplate without tempting despair. She is able only to see it in terms of a dwindling budget, steadily eroding as the costs of health care continue; even the most pressing tasks undone for lack of stamina to see them through; and pain—recurrent, relentless, mercurial.

Though there are no stanza breaks, marking the whole as an unbroken stream of consciousness, the poem shifts perspective when the speaker recalls articles on time management, with rueful irony realizing that she can make sense of the facilitator's question only by an intellectual exercise that has little to do with her own experience of a life lived so provisionally from day to day. She imagines the concentricity of an orderly life where time may be managed like property—predictable, orderly, partitioned by calendar pages that provide a secure structure within which to live and move with relative certainty. The boundaries of her life, on the other hand, are more confining and more easily breached by surprise attacks of pain or weakness that annul all plans. So she protects herself from the overwhelming prospect of stretches of time too large to manage. Like the wisdom of the twelve-step programs that urge "one day at a time," her wisdom is to partition the day into small segments in order to reduce the threat of "too much responsibility."

This strategy works, for the time being—enough for her to take satisfaction in chronicling how she discovered and adopted it. She learned it in the hospital, presumably in the days when pain was most acute and desperation cresting. Forty-five minutes, she discovered, was a livable duration between medications. So she lived 45 minutes at a time, and learned the practical wisdom of setting achievable goals. That learning has served her reasonably well, it seems. She marks the days and nights with vitamins and supplements and transparent strategies that, despite their implausibility, work for the time being, which is where she lives. The time being, she knows, is what she can claim and manage and even sometimes enjoy.

The vision of living a whole day at a time that concludes the poem is a vision of wholeness laced with the ironic awareness that, relative to the way "other people" live, these devices might seem trivial or ineffectual. Still, to live one day at a time, we also recognize, if we've read around in any wisdom tradition, is a worthy objective. It may be that the facilitator's question is predicated on a notion of health that itself is questionable. The poem's form suggests not only the unbroken momentum of this stream of thought but also a breathless accumulation of memories and images that arise in quick succession, fragments that follow one another in a list that cascades as it falls into successively deeper levels of reflection. Some of the line breaks achieve a particularly vivid sense of the halting reluctance to continue, as if what comes next might be the "too much" that always threatens to overwhelm.

After mentioning "the weeks without the money," for instance, the line stops, giving us a moment to register the dimensions of that particular burden before going on to "or the energy"—a piece of information that both compounds the stress of impoverishment and adds a whole new kind of challenge. Similarly, the next lines confront the matter of moving furniture in increments, as though the thought of each element of the task—the weight of the furniture itself, the full garage, the distance to be traveled—presents its own daunting prospect.

The final lines direct us back to the originating question, arriving at a response that is wry, poignant, realistic, and, in its way, hopeful. The speaker's assessment of her own situation has led her to this place, and, one may infer, given her a vision of a limited life more fully lived. That sense of limited life, and realism about the sustained effort required to "keep on keeping on" is a perspective shared by these and many other poets who find in poetry itself an instrument of renewal and a source of the energy required to keep taking the next step, finding ways to survive, enjoy, and even celebrate one day or hour or moment at a time.

Chapter Nine
Allowing Lament

I would like to step out of my heart
and go walking beneath the enormous sky.
         —Rainer Maria Rilke, "Lament"

"Out of the depths I cry . . ." "Nobody knows my sorrow . . ." "I walk a valley of dead men's bones . . ." The echo of lament sounds its sad note through the history of human suffering, with such power and eloquence, many have come to believe that suffering is a taproot of creativity." In Gide's version of Philoctetes, the wounded and abandoned athlete reflects in the midst of his pain and isolation, "I have learned to express myself better, now that I am no longer with men—and I look to telling the story of my sufferings, and if the phrase were very beautiful I was so much consoled; I even sometimes forgot my sadness by uttering it" (Gide, 18).

In answer to those who affirm this widely accepted idea that articulating suffering confers insight, power, and even healing, we also have testimony like that of Randall Jarrell, who insists, in the wry concluding lines of "90 North": "Pain / comes from the darkness, and we call it wisdom. / It is pain" (Jarrell, 113).

Though it may not be wisdom literature, the literature of pain often takes the shape of prayer. The best of it is not the abject prayer of desperation and fear, but utterance of outrage and honesty and assurance that dares, like Job, to address the Almighty, as sure of entitlement and a hearing as of human impotence. He cries in his misery, "Why is light given to a man whose way is hidden, whom God has hedged in? For my sighing comes instead of my bread, and my groanings are poured out like water. For the thing that I fear comes upon me, and what I dread befalls me" (Job 3:23-25). But with equal force he insists, "For I know that my Redeemer lives" (Job 19:25).

Interestingly, in lament, description—often, lengthy description—precedes petition. Importunate demands like "Hear me!" "Listen to my complaint!" seem, if anything, more urgent than the more logical "Do something!" Long inventories of sufferings pervade Psalms, litanies, epics, the stories of survivors who feel compelled to tell a necessary tale of sorrow, not because it can be assuaged—it often can't—but because it deserves to be told. The main character in Christopher Fry's sprightly play, *The Lady's Not for Burning* declares, as she faces the possibility of her own death,

> . . . the least
> I can do is to fill the curled shell of the world
> With human deep-sea sound, and hold it to
> The ear of God, until he has appetite
> To taste our salt sorrow on his lips. (Fry, 99)

Some believe the Holy One has, in fact, tasted that "salt sorrow." But in times of extremity, even many who believe in the suffering Savior revert to the God of Hebrew Scriptures, or the gods of the pagan world, who seem harsher, less predictable, and more inclined to challenge and make us wrestle than to comfort.

Lament is not always religious, or even spiritual. Sometimes it consists simply of a cry into the darkness, often a question, usually "Why?" Part of the suffering of pain, especially chronic pain, is its theological, sometimes even biological, inexplicability. Much of Sara Teasdale's poetry, written in the course of a life darkened by chronic illness from childhood, assumes this character. Though she is recognized for a corpus of poetry that covers a wide range, the mystery of pain and a pull toward death surfaces in it recurrently. Her simple poem entitled "Pain," written at the age of 36 in 1920, gives words to a moment of bemused lament that looks to the natural world for a sense of what is normal as she grapples with the chronic abnormality of her own suffering (Teasdale, 129).

Pain

Waves are the sea's white daughters,
And raindrops the children of rain,
But why for my shimmering body
Have I a mother like Pain?

Night is the mother of stars,
And wind the mother of foam—
The world is brimming with beauty,
But I must stay at home.

The opening two lines personify the processes of the natural world: all phenomena are "birthed" into being. Sea and rain "give birth" to their local forms of wave and drop. So, by analogy, Pain gives birth to the pain that takes shape in one "shimmering body." The word "shimmering" is arresting here, both for its suggestion of a particular kind of luminous beauty and for its suggestion also of a kind of nervous, flickering sensation. The logic of the "motherhood" trope that governs this and the next stanza where night and wind are also "mothers" to particular natural forms carries with it an acceptance of the inevitability of what is received by generation, a legacy inscribed in biology. No question is asked of God; no moral significance is assigned to the persistent pain that sets the speaker apart from others out in the world. The simplicity and restraint of the poem lend it power: no accusations are made, no thwarted expectations reviewed. The "why" question hovers in open space with a kind of purity in the absence of the philosophical schema that seek to discern a plausible logic to experience. Yet it is more than a rhetorical question; it is posed against the backdrop of the clear, appreciative declaration that "the world is brimming with beauty." The beauty and the pain are observed with similar clinical objectivity, as if to indicate that they exist on equal terms. So the "why" assumes something of the tone of amazement we see in Mary's response to the angel: "How can these things be?" How can beauty and pain co-exist? And how is it that I have my being right at their intersection? The poem's plaintiveness, even in the childlike final line, "I must stay at home," aligns it with the painfully unanswerable questions children ask when bad things happen.

Lucille Clifton's "chemotherapy" condenses the features of lament into nine short lines, barely enough to trace a trajectory of feeling, but sufficient in their brevity and boldness to allow raw cries to grow into plot, and then into prayer (Clifton, *Next*, 58):

> chemotherapy
>
> my hair is pain.
> my mouth is a cave of cries,
> my room is filled with white coats
> shaped like God.
> they are moving their fingers along
> their stethoscopes.
> they are testing their chemical faith.
> chemicals chemicals oh mother mary
> where is your living child?

The first three lines convey the striking authority of one who speaks directly from the energy center of her pain. Generally a humble verb, the "is" in these lines gives us an unsettling measure of the speaker's sense that she has been wholly overtaken by a force that seems not only to assault, but to invade and permeate her very being. The difference between the complaint that "Even my hair hurts" (which my daughter once managed to whisper in the midst of a killer migraine) and "my hair is pain" is subtle, perhaps, but significant: that the pain is noun rather than verb presents it as a fact, likely to last—something experienced not as a stage or a sign, but as an accomplished state. What the speaker has undergone feels as though it has transformed her from one condition of being to another altogether. Her hair and her mouth, intimate and significant features of a woman's physical body and social life, have been subsumed into the darkness of a self no longer in control of the alien body she inhabits.

The "cave of cries" gives a sense of that self as a place of deepening darkness, an interior space that echoes and engulfs.

The third and fourth lines redirect our gaze to the speaker's immediate environment, as though her attention is called forth from the timeless darkness of her pain to the social reality of being observed. But the "white coats" are not people, and this is not a human encounter—not an exchange of cry and comfort, or even of information and response. "Shaped like God," the doctors who stand in her room are mythic figures whose purpose has little connection to her suffering. They move their fingers, but not to touch her or to receive information from her body. Rather they move them in aimless speculation, and—the operative verb—"testing" not the drugs, but their own faith in the drugs. The surprising word "faith" makes us aware of the doctors as people engaged in their own journeys, parallel to, perhaps, but not really merging with the patient's. As she imagines them, they are chillingly distant from her suffering, unavailable for comfort. Caricature though it may be, this sense of unbridgeable distance between patient and doctor arises often enough to recognize it as a dimension of hospital treatment that deserves professional reflection.

The repetition of the word "chemicals" in the final lines dramatically reinforces the speaker's sense of being permeated, saturated, overtaken, and sharpens the logic of the final abject cry to "mother mary." Even there, we may be surprised that the words are not some version of "Help me," but rather an expression of lostness and bewilderment: the "where" suggests that the agony of dislocation is larger even than that of physical pain. The experience of loss of self lies at the heart of this poem, which follows the pattern of many Psalms of lament that cry out from a place of abject despair to a God who seems distant, if not indifferent, but finally turn to address that same God in acknowledgment that the source of comfort may not be outside the suffering itself, but as intimately involved with it as a mother with a feverish child. In the end the speaker recovers her child self in the very act of prayer, and what is lost is found at the very site of loss.

A different dimension of loss comes with inability to do those things in which one has invested time, heart, and training. Loss of mobility, flexibility, clarity of speaking, eye-hand coordination, fine motor skills, or any number of other "ordinary" capacities can be profoundly depressing. Years ago, one of the most moving episodes on the long-running TV series, *M*A*S*H* featured a surgeon's having to decide whether to save the arm or leg of a badly wounded soldier in a combat zone. For a number of reasons, he opted to save the leg, only to discover that the soldier was a concert pianist, for whom total loss of hand function assumed tragic proportions. In the final scene the surgeon sat with him at a piano, encouraging him to play Ravel's compositions for the left hand, hoping he might go on to compose music for one hand. The effort served mostly to underscore the totality of the loss. Such a loss is a kind of death that must and will be grieved. Carolyn Foote's poem "Arthritis" takes account of the toll exacted by a disease that does its damage gradually, making small skills first more arduous and finally impossible (Foote, 12).

Arthritis

Nine fingers stride
across the keyboard
with acceptable skill;
the tenth's a laggard.

There's no chance it will
catch up.

Bach and Buxtehude
flinch in old graves
where my dismal, crooked digit
belongs also.

I'd like to abandon it
on someone's doorsill.

The close focus on the hand in this poem locates the problem with a precision that conveys a certain clinical detachment at the outset; she is an observer, watching the "laggard" digit first matter-of-factly, then prognostically, then with harsh judgment for what it has failed to live up to, and finally, speaking in the first person, with personal repulsion. The progression from objectivity to the very subjective felt reaction at the end of the poem suggests a surfacing of feelings not easy to admit. A part of her own body has become alien to her.

The term "acceptable" in the first stanza already situates the speaker as judge of her hands' performance—a splitting from self that bespeaks a strategy of coping by distancing. Assigning the fingers a will of their own creates an objective distance that allows the speaker to tell "their" story without making it hers.

The second stanza, though similarly matter-of-fact, is weightier than the first—not an observation, but a prophecy and a prognosis. What she sees and names indicates a significant, long-term loss. In imagining the composers whose music she has played "flinching" at her impaired performance, she allows one dimension of that loss, humiliation, to surface. The composers represent, perhaps, the teachers, the audiences, the contest judges she can no longer hope to please. The thought of their recoil puts her back in the place of a child who needs and seeks approval for having practiced and gotten it right. The "wrongness" many are made to feel for impairments or deficits beyond their control echoes in these lines where damage is translated into failure.

The "my" sounds the first note of personal attachment and introduces lament. The "dismal, crooked digit" is still named as a thing apart, whose fate the speaker can still regard as a thing apart from her observing self, but that distance begins to close with the possessive pronoun.

The idea that that lagging finger belongs in its own grave, bizarre as it seems, transitions to the dark ending of the poem where disgust, disappointment, and deep frustration emerge from behind the veil of detachment. The fantasy of abandoning the arthritic digit "on someone's doorsill" evokes at least two harsh associations: an abandoned child left to the care of strangers, or, more brutally, an object left where it will be stepped on and crushed. The flicker of pity suggested in "dismal" has turned to anger and rejection of the offending part. "If thine eye offend thee, pluck it out," reads one of the more disconcert-ing admonitions in scripture, suggesting what radical action may be required to reject temptation and moral offense. Here, the damage comes to signify an offense curiously assigned "moral" significance, deserving amputation from the body and burial or abandonment. Anger, of course, is one face of grief. The speaker's anger here comes not from arthritic pain, but from the loss of a life-giving skill. The poem allows us to see how what might seem a minor disability relative to many others might be a costly and life-changing loss.

The lives of disabled people can easily become defined by losses, their narratives expansions upon litanies prohibition: what they cannot do may become, not only for those who see them in terms of their disability, but for the disabled as well, the defining feature of their stories. It is hard work to devise alternative narratives. Lament has to precede such a project, as grief has to precede fully recovery from bereavement. Real lament is its own art form; deeper and more ontological than self-pity, often couched in specifically spiritual terms such as prayer, lament is a cry of the heart and an effort to engage in truth-telling, to set the record straight before God and the world, to recognize human helplessness and reckon with it. Authentic lament often breaches boundaries of decorum, re-spectability, popular piety; in includes outrage as well as sorrow. "Forbidden," a prose-poem by Justine Blevins, confined to a wheelchair for many years, pro-vides a list of "wants" framed by the title word that suggests that the restrictions she lives with are not simply "bad luck," but in some unspecified way a function of willed prohibition; she not only cannot, but may not participate with normal ease of access in experiences that are freely available to others (Blevins, unpub). What gives the list its power is partly its psychological complexity, mixing as it does conflicting desires—for self-destruction, self-fulfillment, freedom, attach-ment, wildness, submissiveness—and partly its form—an unbroken stream of desires separated only by commas, tumbling out one after the other with no excuses or explanations, no modification or modulation.

Forbidden

what I want:

to kill myself take lots of pills to scream and yell and cry and sleep
and kiss and make love and dive in the ocean to feel loved and cherished
and snuggle up next to a warm body , hold someone close to my heart, to
feel electric, to be wild, free, listen to poetry read by a lover, run my
fingers through his hair, touch, gaze, absorb, laugh, rest, speak aloud
without fear, fly a kite, hold a baby, jetski and fall in the water, feel
the texture of bark , of his skin , a thorn, the silk of rose petal, eyes
not hesitant , no questions, only passion yearning desire consumed by
fire , kiss underwater, hold hands watching the sunset, to be needed, a
vixen, a scholar, a teacher , to tackle someone in anger, passion, play,
to be heard respected to break windows with bare fists and watch as my
own blood runs because I am alive, to run in the rain , get caught in
lightning , to lay in the sand and feel its grainy texture, to lay in the
grass and feel it tickle and scratch , stretching like a cat languorous to
be dangerous and feared , sensual and sensuous, to fire a gun and feel its
kick, fly an airplane, burn pages and pages, ripped into jagged cutting
edges and throw them off the cliff, drive a race car, have the breath
stolen from my lungs, stare up at the night sky, sleep in satin sheets,
wear a teddy rip his shirt watch buttons fly hear them pop, with my teeth,
slow, snaking down massage oil hot slippery skin

This simple but searing inventory of "forbidden" pleasures is striking in its
"ordinariness." The reasons they are "forbidden" vary, and are worth reflec-
tion. Some represent pleasures that are simply impossible for a person with
reduced mobility—jet skiing, swimming in the ocean, flying an airplane. Some
are pleasures less accessible because those who are disabled are put at a serious
disadvantage in a culture that so loudly and incessantly reinforces standards
of sexual appeal and acceptability that are hard for any but a fraction of the
population to meet. They live among people conditioned to avert their gaze,

most unlikely to recognize the desirability of a woman in a wheelchair without some added motive to look longer than most. Some are forbidden because they take too much help, effort, expense, because the lives of the disabled are costly as well as constrained.

To name the range of things one can't have is one way of staking out the territory of illness. Before that restricted field can be domesticated into living space, the boundaries must be drawn, the barbed wire strung. The speaker takes stock, beginning with "to kill myself," following that desire with a host of desires that belie it. She wants the life of the body—sex, sports, naked contact with the textures of the physical world—and a purposeful life of the mind—scholar, teacher. She wants emotions many disabled people feel are forbidden because of a particular pressure to please others in hope of not being ignored. She wants risk and a bit of riotous living. That want is affirmed and discussed with compassion on a number of websites, including that of the National Sexuality Resource Center (www.nsrc.sfsu.edu), where the point is simply made that "All too often, people with disabilities are desexualized by doctors, care-givers, friends, family—and in many cases— themselves."

The sorrow of forfeited or circumscribed sexual expression is a common focus of lament, though it is a form of suffering whose naming is as likely to incite embarrassment as empathy. Post-mastectomy poems in particular frequently identify this dimension of loss as the most tragic. The poems themselves are acts of courage; in bringing to light their sadness in feeling they have lost sexual appeal, women have to get past the shame that would incite them to hide that loss behind veils of clothing and silence. Wanda Coleman's poem, "Mastectomy" is typical of this kind of courageous self-exposure. Known as "the L.A. blues-woman" and by some as "the unofficial poet laureate of Los Angeles," Coleman writes with a strong sense of how women, and in a particular way African-American women still speak from the margins of a culture where being white, young, beautiful in prescribed ways and able-bodied is normative (Coleman, 148). In a 2010 interview with Amber Mosure in *Superstition Review* she observed that there were still, in this culture, strong "taboos against women being angry, even when justified, and against expressions of non-exploitive eroticism from women (Coleman, online). The title of this poem challenges that taboo, and challenges readers to look directly at a fact about women's lives and desires from which the public gaze is politely averted.

mastectomy

the fall of
velvet plum points and umber aureolae
remember living
forget cool evening air kisses the rush of
liberation freed from the brassiere
forget the cupping of his hands the pleasure
his eyes looking down/anticipating
forget his mouth. his tongue at the nipples
his intense hungry nursing
forget sensations which begin either
on the right or the left. go thru the body
linger between thighs
forget the space once grasped during his ecstasy
sweet sweet mama you taste so

The poem's opening line casts a wide net, evoking with the word "fall" an analogy between mastectomy and the fall of fruit, the fall of idols or ideals, the fall from grace, "fall" being an archetypal situation and story line.

The second reinforces the image of fruit, to which breasts are often compared, but also takes away the veil of metaphor in the word "aureolae," offering the breast itself to the reader's imagination—its color, its shape, its texture. Its frankness is offset by the deliberate devices of alliteration and assonance that make the line as much as the image a focus of interest—a poet's reminder that the telling is as important as, and inseparable from, what is told.

The ambiguity of this line, set alone in open space, works in two grammatically possible ways. The first continues the sentence begun in the opening lines, claiming that the body remembers, vividly and tragically in the ache of "phantom limbs," or, in her case a phantom breast, and in the way nerves, cells, and brain record the insults it receives. The second is as an imperative—a command to the self to remember how to live, find some deeper memory of living than the memories of sensations now lost with the amputated breast—the way it felt opened to evening air upon disrobing, the lover's touch and gaze, the way orgasm traveled from the breasts throughout the body.

As in Blevins' poem, "Forbidden," a good part of this poem is an enumeration of what may no longer be taken for granted as a rightful and normal human pleasure. The words of the poem take us through the stages of sexual encounter, each moment of it to be separately mourned and relinquished. In keeping with that schema, the final line is left unfinished, perhaps to suggest the way words give way to gasps of ecstasy or simply to deep, encompassing silence in the act of love, but perhaps also to signify the truncation, the loss of completeness and completion that seem impossible now.

The paradox of lamentation is that when it serves its clearest purposes it underscores both the uniqueness of each person's suffering and the way in which suffering unites us to others—to all who have felt pain, loss, or sorrow, to all who have found in the life of the fragile and damaged body moments of spiritual encounter that may leave them limping like Jacob but that also open a way to costly understanding. When that understanding is shared, it helps equip the rest of us for our own inevitable relinquishments.

Chapter Ten
At the Threshold

Because I could not stop for Death,
He kindly stopped for me.
                    —Emily Dickinson

Among Bach's gentlest and most dignified choral works is the slow, meditative *Komm, süßer Tod* ("Come, Sweet Death," trans. online). The music elevates and enriches the lyrics' full and frank acknowledgement that longing for death is a common human desire, not always born of depression or what we might call self-destructive fantasies, but from the mere fact that life may become wearisome and burdensome, that suffering can exhaust the last resources of body and spirit, that age is not always or altogether a blessing. The words are a prayer, not an outcry like Job's, not a rejection of life, but a confession of readiness to lay down this life in hope of whatever peace may come thereafter.

> Come, sweet death, come blessed rest!
> Come lead me to peace
> for I am weary of the world,
> oh come! I wait for you,
> come soon and lead me,
> close my eyes.
> Come, blessed rest!

The spirit of this first stanza continues through the remaining four. Death is personified as a benevolent guide who may come to see us through the last great transition. More than acceptance, this lovely song looks toward death with welcome and hope.

By one estimate, only about 19% of Americans die what may still be called "natural" deaths in old age. Many die violently in accidents or war zones; many die early of cancer or heart disease. Only a minority have the opportunity to live long enough and fully enough to be ready and eager for closure. Those who die of prolonged illness have time to foresee and reflect on their own departure—an opportunity some still regard as a blessing—and to go through a process of arriving at acceptance, relinquishment and peace.

Keats' sonnet, "When I have fears that I may cease to be," written not long before the medically trained poet died at 26 of tuberculosis, has provided generations of readers one durable model of that process (Keats, 776). In it the poet reasons his way through fear of death, emerging finally into a cosmic perspective that brings him peace:

> When I have fears that I may cease to be
> Before my pen has glean'd my teeming brain,
> Before high pil'd books, in charact'ry,
> Hold like rich garners the full-ripen'd grain;
> When I behold, upon the night's starr'd face,
> Huge cloudy symbols of a high romance,
> And feel that I may never live to trace
> Their shadows, with the magic hand of chance;
> And when I feel, fair creature of an hour!
> That I shall never look upon thee more,
> Never have relish in the faery power
> Of unreflecting love;—then on the shore
>   Of the wide world I stand alone, and think,
>   Till Love and Fame to nothingness do sink.

Three fears assail him—that he will not live long enough to bring his gifts to fruition, that he will not live to experience the adventure promised young men, that he will never again see the face of his beloved. His escape from these fears lies in solitary reflection from the "shore / of the wide world"—a perspective from which human life looks small and human ambition insignificant. Respite and resolution come by widening the frame to what some might call a heavenly or cosmic perspective.

This release from fear, earthly ambitions and preoccupations, and loss of love and life is recorded in a rich legacy of poetry by people facing death. Contemporary poems of that genre are less likely than those of a few generations ago to express traditional religious hope or even to focus on afterlife, but most trace a journey toward acceptance and peace, though it may take them along perilous paths of complex sorrow.

An untitled poem by Susan Rothstein, who died at the age of 51 in 2002 speaks in the voice of one who has consciously taken on this final challenge, learned from it, and knows she has something to teach (Rothstein, unpub). Her approach to readers is to explain how it is to be living in the end stages of cancer, gently correcting those who may regard her with misplaced pity, helping to prepare those who will one day have to walk this hard road as well.

> When you are 49
> and your body is
> riddled with cancer
> You stop holding back much
>   It's easy to write a poem
> because you have nothing to fear
>   The imagined evaluation of others
> has become a soundless
> wisp of weak wind –
>   And what you hear is only your own heart
> beating out its steady song -
> This is your life
> This is your life
> The whole of life sucks down
> with a thunderous, swooshing swirl
> into a minute -
> breath going in
> breath going out
>   I get up each day and think

who will I love today?
I do not think of death
except as a place of rest
my body accepts who it is
　　　Finally, underneath
I know this is as natural
as natural gets
despite chemo, lasers and pills
decay, deformity
and odd twists
　　　Fill the forests and fields
and hospital waiting rooms
with gentle eyed creatures
whose souls know
There was never any promise given
and what you have is a morning
eyes to see
ears to hear
heart to feel
hands to touch
mind to bend down in humble amazement
at what has been given

The simple, short lines of this poem with their approximate symmetries map a breath-like rhythm: in-out, systole-diastole, slight irregularities absorbed in the persistent succession of phrase upon phrase.

The "you" opens the poem as a general explanation of what the world looks like from this particular place—at 49, riddled with cancer. It is a place from which the speaker can speak with the peculiar authority conferred by experience, the authority of the autobiographer who knows her purposes—to teach, to disclose, to explain, to encourage.

Nothing left to fear is a place of liberation, not easy to speak of, since it would be glib for anyone but the patient to acknowledge that dying may be liberating. The logic of these lines suggests that the poem itself is an act of freedom and an act of courage—that a poem like this is a thing achieved only after one has been willing to accept the hardest truths, and has seen bedrock.

The freedom of knowing one is going to die releases one from various anxieties. Fear of judgment, a persistent anxiety for many people, may be one of the last to go; now, though, courtesies and precautionary behaviors fall away. One's sense of accountability shifts: fidelity to one's own deepest purposes trumps all superficial concerns. The wide popularity of the cheerful poem, "When I am an Old Woman I shall Wear Purple" suggests how many may long for just such release from social judgment: when death is nearer, one can afford to be amused.

Every spiritual tradition teaches some practice of living in the moment, focusing on breath, being mindful, being present, taking no thought for the morrow, being like the lilies of the field, knowing that life is fleeting. It is not inevitable, but also not unusual for those who know they are near death to experience what the speaker describes here: the concentration of a whole life into the time one has—in Eliot's words, knowing that "all is always now."

The "to do" list for the speaker in this poem has dissolved into an open-ended willingness to love those life presents her with. She accepts the loss of occupation and of the identity that goes with it. She accepts death. She accepts her diminishing body. Interestingly she makes the body the subject of its own clause: the body has to release its own resistances.

In *How We Die* Sherwin Nuland discusses the ways North American medical culture prevents most patients from dying natural deaths. Efforts to cure often persist to the point of diminishing returns, he points out, partly because we have opened up wide grey areas where "living" can be technologically prolonged. Sometimes those efforts result in actual healing and longer living. But to this speaker cure is an idea whose time has gone. That death is "as natural / as natural gets" is a deep comfort now. The process has begun, and the knowing that comes with it.

The shift into the imperative raises the register of the poem suddenly, with a heightened certainty of purpose. "Fill the forests and fields / and hospital waiting rooms" is an appeal for a return and a renewal of that knowing. Creatures who accept death live peaceably in a way we cannot when we fight too hard.

It is an appeal to recognize the terms on which life was given—the spiritual contract by which we live: that "There was never any promise given" of length of days or durability of health or dreams fulfilled. But to get to be human, the gift of life itself, may be received even on harder terms than we may think we are capable of accepting. The speaker's acceptance carries the authority of one who stands at the final threshold. From any other point of view, it would be pious theorizing. But to say yes to death when you are looking at it directly and at close range confers a right to stare it down and walk peaceably in its shadow.

Some patients set up camp very near that threshold and dwell there for some time. Some who live with cancer or AIDS or MS or any of a range of degenerative diseases find themselves living the paradox—that all who live are dying—with a clarity and immediacy that challenges the very idea of "ordinary."

"Terminal" and "chronic" are sometimes nearly indistinguishable. In that condition one has time to adapt to the thought of death: dread or fear may fade some days into tedium or may be overshadowed by small pleasures or may recede to a distance from which one can consider them critically, imaginatively, even playfully. Roberta de Kay, one of the many patients who worked with John Fox in the writing groups represented in *Poetic Medicine*, approaches the thought of her own death speculatively, with a whimsy that is similar in its affirmation of freedom and release to Susan Rothstein's. Without attachment to any traditional notion of heaven or afterlife, she entertains a range of possibilities, each of which has a visceral appeal, each of which domesticates death by analogy, metaphor, or image, making it not so very different from the transitions we witness along the way (de Kay, 180).

Maybe

Maybe we dance from this elegant place
    discarding our vulnerable bodies
        like old workclothes at the end of the day.

Maybe essence enters the air flying
    like monarchs in migration past roses
        and rivers older than wood wizards.

Maybe meaning and magic stand up from
the landscape like summer lightning,
and for one holy moment

All questions have answers, all journeys a home,
all living roundness and warmth
of a stone clutched tight in the hand.

Or maybe like four-year-olds we
drop everything and simply run forward
dazzled again!

The idea of the body as a garment to be shed may be limited and limiting, given the ways mystery of the mind-body relationship deepens with every advance in mind-brain research, but the notion has a venerable history, and for good reason. However one assesses the credibility of near-death stories about soul travel, out-of-body experience, or language about passing over into the light, the volume of such testimony suggests how common and comforting is the idea that when the body is "shed," like old clothing, like the skin of a snake, like the woven cocoon, one "goes on." When the body becomes emaciated, impotent, incompetent, painful, it is easy to imagine that leaving it behind would be a joyful release.

Flying, too is an archetypal dream image that suggests empowerment, widened vision, and release from earthly attachment. The popular funeral song (often sung or played as a "second line" piece, as attendees emerge from the funeral back into the immediacies of community life), "I'll fly away" is one of many exuberant appropriations of flying as an image of hope:

I'll Fly Away

Some glad morning when this life is o'er,
I'll fly away;
To a home on God's celestial shore,
I'll fly away (I'll fly away).

Chorus:
I'll fly away, Oh Glory
I'll fly away; (in the morning)
When I die, Hallelujah, by and by,
I'll fly away (I'll fly away).
2.
When the shadows of this life have gone,
I'll fly away;
Like a bird from prison bars has flown,
I'll fly away (I'll fly away)
3.
Just a few more weary days and then,
I'll fly away;
To a land where joy shall never end,
I'll fly away (I'll fly away)

Interestingly, this funeral song with its lively beat is not about the one who has gone, but about the hope of the living who one day will join the dead. The images of butterfly and bird, suggesting beauty, power, freedom and transformation, inhabitants of air as well as earth help transform grief and dread to a hope that, for many, is very real. Roberta de Kay adds to it the idea of "migration," a way of going home that is natural, instinctive, and sure. Migration changes the idea of loss into one of deep, slow rhythmic exchange of one good for another. The butterfly she mentions passes roses and rivers, not stopping where it might once have alighted, being now about some other business.

In this poem, too, the hope of enlightenment as a gift death brings is made lively as "summer lightning"—sudden, epiphanic, exciting, instantaneous, whole, and also, again, natural. The biblical promise that "in the twinkling of an eye" we shall be changed (I Cor. 15:52) echoes in the poet's speculation that the final paradigm shift will occur with a suddenness that precludes all reasoning, effortless, given, palpable as a stone in the hand, welcome as warmth, complete.

The final image of the poem—of a four-year-old dropping everything and running forward, dazzled—echoes another biblical idea: we must "become like little children" to "enter the kingdom of heaven." Reclaiming a state not simply of innocence, but of openness, readiness for surprise, curiosity, and the unquestioned sense of being accepted and welcome that comes with a healthy childhood comports with the notion of "shedding" in the opening stanza. What must be shed are the acquired inhibitions, doubts, paralyzing rationalizations, pedantic quibblings that may keep us from seeing and saying yes to personal revelation that summons us to respond.

Commenting on her own poem, de Kay writes, "I imagine now that in dying, whenever that comes in my life, there will be yet more meaning to discover." There is no philosophical or theological certainty in this statement of hope, just a resting in what imagination can provide. Acceptance of one's own death can teach this kind of negative capability—the capacity to dwell in paradox or uncertainty without, as Keats put it, "straining after resolution."

That quality of acceptance is as beautifully articulated in Jane Kenyon's much-beloved poem, "Let Evening Come"—a poem that draws a part of its considerable power from the rich ambiguity of the imperative "let,"—both concession and command (Kenyon, 69). The poem was written for a friend who was dying of cancer even as she also knew she was very likely dying as well.

As in de Kay's poem, the speaker moves through a succession of images, each one allowing a new level of awareness and acceptance, like a litany in which a single focus is held through a succession of images or names, each of which offers a slight shift of frame.

Let Evening Come

Let the light of late afternoon
shine through chinks in the barn, moving
up the bales as the sun moves down.

Let the cricket take up chafing
as a woman takes up her needles
and her yarn. Let evening come.

Let dew collect on the hoe abandoned
in long grass. Let the stars appear
and the moon disclose her silver horn.

Let the fox go back to its sandy den.
Let the wind die down. Let the shed
go black inside. Let evening come.

To the bottle in the ditch, to the scoop
in the oats, to air in the lung
let evening come.

Let it come, as it will, and don't
be afraid. God does not leave us
comfortless, so let evening come.

The speaker's close attention to the light of late afternoon in the opening stanza suggests an acute and palpable sense of how time wreaks its changes, and how those change are not all diminishment, but rather exchange of one form of beauty for another. The opening phrase, "Let the light" evokes God's "Let there be light" in a way that situates the speaker as co-creator by means of her consent to what is and must be. The second stanza adds hearing to seeing, and offers generous recognition to the creatures whose work is comparable to that of humans who know their daily tasks and tend them. Thus the wild harbingers of nighttime are domesticated and welcomed. Then, in the third, inanimate objects are included in the general grace of permission and blessing, as though to say with St. Thomas that "Everything that is, is good"—the whole created order, natural and manufactured, has an order and rightness despite our many ways of disrupting it, that even in times of extremity can be reaffirmed: dew falls; stars appear; day ends. The following stanza introduces relinquishment—all things return from the occupations of this life to their hiding places, rest, quiescence, darkness.

Then the poem shifts a little, moving our focus from subjects to objects: evening comes to each person and thing discretely. It comes to all things hollow—the bottle, the scoop, the lungs—filling with darkness what is emptied of light. That the lungs are merely mentioned here as an item on the list of spaces to be entered emphasizes not only the naturalness, but the ordinariness of encroaching darkness.

The final stanza seems to take another quarter turn to face the reader directly with a word that is both directive and prophetic, fraught with a certain urgency even in its calm assurance: "Let it come as it will and don't / be afraid." Again and again wisdom traditions underscore this word of instruction as a way of liberation—do not be afraid. Fear not—followed often by a promise like the one the angel gives to Mary—"for behold, I bring you tidings of great joy"—or the one the poet gives here: "God will not leave us comfortless."

In light of that promise, the final words ring with a new level of acceptance or readiness. The poem, like a prayer, expunges the boundaries between the physical and spiritual dimensions, invoking perhaps the oldest image of death, the end of day. But in the Jewish tradition that harks back to Genesis' "and the evening and the morning were the first day," evening is both an ending and a beginning. Sabbath begins at twilight. Though Kenyon's poem makes no mention of the "morning" into which some hope to "fly away," the quiet hope in the double negative of the last stanza, "God will not leave us comfortless," is enough, she suggests, for now. Her uncertainty, like that of de Kay's "maybe" is not a restless, anxious wondering, but a place of repose. Childlike, she believes that both the one dying and the one left will have what they need.

Works Cited

Chapter One

Anne Hunsaker Hawkins, *Reconstructing Illness: Studies in Pathography* (West Lafayette, IN: Purdue University Press, 1993).

Gillie Bolton, "Every Poem Breaks a Silence that Had to Be Overcome: The Therapeutic Value of Poetry Writing," *Feminist Review*, No. 62, *Contemporary Women Poets* (Summer, 1999) pp. 118-133.

Barbara Neri, "The Consolation of Poetry" TDR (1988-), Vol. 47, No. 3 (Autumn, 2003), pp. 45-77.

John Fox, *Poetic Medicine: The Healing Art of Poem-Making* (NY: Jeremy Tarcher/Putnam, 1997).

Larry Dossey, *Space, Time, and Medicine* (Shambala Press, 1982).

Rafael Campo. *The Healing Art: A Doctor's Black Bag of Poetry.* New York: W. W. Norton, 2003.

Karen Fiser, "Still Life with Open Window," *Losing and Finding* (Denton: U North Texas Press, 2003).

Mary Bradish O'Connor, "Midnight Cancer," *Say Yes Quickly* (Comptche, CA: Pot Shard Press, 1997).

Mandy Richmond Dowd, "Out in the Sun the Busy Lives Swirl," unpublished, 1992.

Chapter Two

Peter Meinke, "The Patient," *The Night Train and the Golden Bird*, University of Pittsburgh Press, 1977.

T.S. Eliot, "East Coker," *Four Quartets* (NY: Harcourt, Brace, Jovanovich, 1943, 1971).

Linda Pastan, "Migraine," *An Early Afterlife* (NY: W.W. Norton, 1995).

Wyatt Prunty, "Emaciated Poetry," *Sewanee Review*, Vol. 93, No. 1, Winter 1985.

Jane Kenyon, "Now Where," *Otherwise* (St. Paul, MN: Greywolf Press, 1996).

Jane Kenyon, "Afternoon in the House," *Otherwise* (Greywolf, 1996).

Kathleen Norris, *Acedia and Me: A Marriage, Monks, and a Writer's Life* (Riverhead, 2008).

Annie Stenzel, "An Incantation for the Small Hours of the Night," *Academic Medicine*, Vol. 82, Issue 3, March 2007.

Chapter Three

Anne Sexton, "The Abortion," *The Complete Poems: Anne Sexton* (NY: Mariner Books, 1999).

B.A. St. Andrews (Bonnie), "Oncological Cocktails," *Journal of General Internal Medicine*, Volume 13 (8) Springer Journals – Aug 1, 1998.

B.A. St. Andrews, http://www.upstate.edu/bioethics/thehealingmuse/founded.php

B.A. St. Andrews, www.upstate.edu/bioethics/thehealingmuse.

Gilda Radner, *It's Always Something* (NY: Simon and Schuster, 1989).

Ralph W. Moss, *The Cancer Industry* (Equinox Press, 1996).

Patricia Goedicke, "In the Hospital," *Her Soul Beneath the Bone: Women's Poetry on Breast Cancer* (U Illinois Press, 1988).

Ron Slate, "On the Seawall: Ron Slate's Website," Feb. 9, 2008: http://www.ronslate.com/baseball_field_night_last_poems_patricia_goedicke_lost_horses_press

Lynn Payer, *Medicine and Culture* (Hoit Paperbacks, 1996).

Chapter Four

The British Medical Journal, Dec. 30, 1871.

Alice Jones, "The Biopsy," *The Knot* (Cambridge, MA: Alice James Books, 1992), p. 43-44.

Chana Bloch, "In the Land of the Body," *The Past Keeps Changing* (NY: The Sheepmeadow Press, 1992).

T.S. Eliot, *The Waste Land and Other Poems* (NY: Harcourt, Brace & Co., 1934, 1962).

Nikola Biller-Andorno and Henning Schauenburg, "It's Only Love? Some Pitfalls in Emotionally Related Organ Donation," *Journal of Medical Ethics*, Vol. 27, No. 3, June 2001.

Lucille Clifton, "donor," *Blessing the Boats: New and Selected Poems 1988-2000*

(Rochester, NY: BOA Editions, Ltd., 2000).

Lucille Clifton, text of recorded interview at: http://www.gracecavalieri.com/ significantPoets/lucilleClifton.html

William Matthews, "Recovery Room," *Search Party: Collected Poems of William Matthews* (NY: Houghton Mifflin Co., 2004).

Susan Sontag, *Illness as Metaphor* (NY: Farrar, Strauus and Giroux, 1978).

Chapter Five

Beverlye Hyman Fead, "Vulnerable," *I Can Do This: Living with Cancer, Tracing a Year of Hope* (Santa Barbara Cancer Wellness Program Publishing, 2004).

Adam Mars-Jones, "Slim," *The Darker Proof: Stories from a Crisis* (London: Faber and Faber, 1987).

Lynn Goldfarb, "Still," in *Claiming the Spirit Within*, Marilyn Sewell, ed. (Boston: Beacon Press, 1996).

Simmons Buntin, "Interview with Sandra Steingraber," Terrain.org Interviews: http://www.terrain.org/interview/20/

Sandra Steingraber, "Waiting for the Lab Reports, Thinking of Penelope," *Post-Diagnosis*, (Ithaca, NY: Firebrand Books, 1995).

Eamon Grennan, "Diagnosis," *Kenyon Review*; Fall 89, Vol. 11 Issue 4. Also in *As If it Matters* (Greywolf Press, 1992).

Lucille Clifton, "cancer," *Mercy* (BOA Editions, 2004).

Deena Metzger, "I Am No Longer Afraid," *Tree: Essays and Pieces* (North Atlantic Books, 1997). Also at http://www.deenametzger.com/

Deena Metzger, http://www.deenametzger.com/healing/Thinking%20About%20 Healing.htm

Chapter Six

Flannery O'Connor, *The Habit of Being: Letters of Flannery O'Connor* (NY: Farrar, Straus and Giroux, 1988).

D.H. Lawrence, "Malade," *The Complete Poems of D.H. Lawrence* (NY: Viking Press, 1964, 1971).

Nancy Mairs, "Diminishment," *With Wings: An Anthology of Literature by and about Women with Disabilities* (NY: Feminist Press, 1987).

Nancy Mairs, "On Being a Cripple," *Plain Text* (Tucson: U Arizona Press, 1986).

Diana Neutze, website: http://mylivinganddying.com/about.php

Nancy Louise Peterson, "I Entered the Room, Naked," *The Cancer Poetry Project: Poems by Cancer Patients and Those Who Love Them*, Karin Miller, ed. (Minneapolis, MN: Tasora Books, 2001).

William Shakespeare, *King Lear* Act III, sc. 4, l. 105-7.

Chapter Seven

Harold Bond "The Game," *Despite This Flesh: The Disabled in Stories and Poems*, ed. Vassar Miller (Austin: U Texas, 1985).

Miller book summary: http://www.amazon.com/Despite-this-Flesh-Disabled- Stories/ dp/0292715501/ref=sr_1_1?s=books&ie=UTF8&qid=1339177312&sr=1-1

Eric Berne, *Games People Play* (NY: Ballantine Books, 1996).

Floyd Skloot, "Home Remedies," *Journal of the American Medical Association, July 1991; 266.*

Elizabeth Jennings, "Diagnosis," *Timely Issues* (Manchester, UK: Carcanet Press, 2001).

Murielle Minard, "Bedtime Story," *With Wings: An Anthology of Literature by and about Women with Disabilities*, eds. Marsha Saxton and Florence Howe (NY: Feminist Press, 1987).

Chapter Eight

Lucille Clifton, *the terrible stories* (Brockport, NY: BOA Editions, 1996).

Margalit Fox, obituary in *New York Times*, February 17, 2010.

Gayle Sulik, *Pink Ribbon Blues*, (Oxford UP, 2010), Chapter 8, quoted at http:// gaylesulik.com/2010/12/the-terrible-stories/

Lucille Clifton, "dialysis" *Blessing the Boats: New and Selected Poems 1988-2000* (Rochester, NY: BOA Editions, 2000).

Toni Morrison, *Beloved* (NY: Knopf, 1987).

Margaret Robison, "Five Months After My Stroke," Sue Brannan Walker and Rosely Rosfman, eds., *Life on the Line: Selections on Words and Healing* (Negative Capability Press, 1992), p. 224.

Richard Hugo, "Hot Springs" from *The Lady in Kicking Horse Reservoir* (Carnegie Mellon University Press, 1999).

Barbara Ruth, "In My Disabled Women's Group," *With Wings: An Anthology of Lierature By and About Women with Disabilities*, ed. Marsha Saxton and Florence Howe (NY: Feminist Press, 1987).

Chapter Nine

André Gide, trans., *Philoctetes*, quoted in Philip Sandblom, *Illness and Creativity* (Philadelphia: George Stickley Co., 1982).

Randall Jarrell, "90 North," *Randall Jarrell: The Complete Poems* (NY: Farrar, Straus and Giroux, 1981).

Christopher Fry, *The Lady's Not for Burning* (Dramatists' Play Service, Inc., 1948, 53).

Sara Teasdale, "Pain," *Collected Poems of Sara Teasdale* (NY: Macmillan, 1974).

Lucille Clifton, "chemotherapy," *Next: New Poems* (Boa Editions, 1989).

Carolyn Foote, "Arthritis," *With Wings: An Anthology of Lit by and about Women with Disabilities*, eds. Marsha Saxton and Florence Howe (NY: Feminist Press, 1987.

Justine Blevins, "Forbidden" (Santa Barbara, unpublished poem).

Wanda Coleman, interview with Amber Mosure in *Superstition Review*, Feb. 28, 2010 at http://kalamu.posterous.com/interview-wanda-coleman.

Wanda Coleman, "Mastectomy," *In Whatever Houses We May Visit: Poems That Have Inspired Physicians*, Michael LaCombe and Thomas V. Hartman, eds. (American College of Physicians, 2008). Also at http://www.poets.org/viewmedia.php/prmMID/15534

Chapter Ten

Johann Sebastian Bach, German and English lyrics at: http://www2.cpdl.org/wiki/
index.php/Komm,_s%C3%BCsser_Tod_%28Johann_Sebastian_Bach%29

John Keats, "When I Have Fears that I May Cease to Be," *The Norton Anthology of
English Literature*, 6th Edition, Vol. 2 (NY: W.W. Norton, 1993).

Susan Rothstein, untitled, unpublished poem, provided by Lena Rothstein, San
Francisco, CA.

Roberta de Kay, "Maybe" John Fox, *Poetic Medicine* (Jeremy Tarcher/Putnam,
1997).

Albert E. Brumley, "I'll Fly Away" (Hartford Music Company, 1932).

Jane Kenyon, "Let Evening Come," *Let Evening Come* (St. Paul: Greywolf Press,
1990).

Permissions

"Still Life with Open Window" by Karen Fiser from *Losing and Finding*. Copyright © 2003 by Karen Fiser. Reprinted with the poet's permission.

Untitled, unpublished poem by Susan. Reprinted with permission from Kenneth Rothstein.

"Vulnerable," unpublished poem by Beverlye Hyman Fead. Reprinted with the poet's permission.

"Waiting for the Lab Reports, Thinking of Penelope," by Sandra Steingraber from *Post-Diagnosis*. Copyright © by Sandra Steingraber, 1995. Reprinted with permission from Charlotte Sheedy Literary Agency.